THE LITTLE BOOK

OF

BEHAVIORAL
INVESTING

Little Book Big Profits Series

In the *Little Book Big Profits* series, the brightest icons in the financial world write on topics that range from tried-and-true investment strategies to tomorrow's new trends. Each book offers a unique perspective on investing, allowing the reader to pick and choose from the very best in investment advice today.

Books in the *Little Book Big Profits* series include:

The Little Book That Beats the Market by Joel Greenblatt
The Little Book of Value Investing by Christopher Browne
The Little Book of Common Sense Investing by John C. Bogle
The Little Book That Makes You Rich by Louis Navellier
The Little Book That Builds Wealth by Pat Dorsey
The Little Book That Saves Your Assets by David M. Darst
The Little Book of Bull Moves in Bear Markets by Peter D. Schiff
The Little Book of Main Street Money by Jonathan Clements
The Little Book of Safe Money by Jason Zweig
The Little Book of Behavioral Investing by James Montier

THE LITTLE BOOK

OF

BEHAVIORAL
INVESTING

How Not to Be Your Own

Worst Enemy

JAMES MONTIER

WILEY

John Wiley & Sons, Inc.

ISBN 978-0-470-68602-7

Printed in the United States of America

10 9 8 7 6

To Charlotte
Your smile lights up my world

Contents

Foreword

Homo Mistakus

I AM RATHER AN EXPERT ON BAD CHOICES. I have made so many over the years, from unhealthy food choices to postponing exercise (today's bad choice) and yes, even regrettable investment choices (sigh).

And then I have observed so many bad choices on the part of my seven teenagers. (Thankfully, now down to just one, but these days I get to watch my grandkids learn to navigate the world.) Teenagers have a remarkable ability to make the easy choice today and postpone the hard and difficult choice until tomorrow. And some of us grow up, having perfected that ability, making even more bad choices as adults.

I have interviewed hundreds of investors over the years, from small and starting out to having-arrived billionaires. I am always amazed by the mistakes they make and the inventive rational they use for having made them.

As a nation and a world, we have made numerous bad choices, taken the easy road, and ended up in the worst global economic crisis in 80 years. Now we are faced with a set of difficult choices as we work our way back to a new normal. History is replete with bad choices by both individuals and nations.

In the past few decades, a new science has emerged that has taken note of the fact that not only are we sometimes irrational, but we are predictably irrational. This new behavioral science has started looking at how we go about making decisions and is finding all sorts of interesting, if sometimes distressing, things about the human species.

It seems that our emotions and much of our decision-making process is hard wired into our brains, developed for survival on the African savannahs some 100,000 years ago. We adapted to movement, learning to make decisions quickly, because there was quite a difference, literally life and death, between dodging dangerous lions and chasing succulent antelope.

And while those survival instincts are quite useful in general, when translated into a modern world, and especially a modern investment world, they make us prone to all sorts of errors. Think of chasing momentum all too often in the hope that it will continue and running from falling markets just as they start to turn. What works for survival in the African jungles is not as productive in the jungles of world finance.

Happily, we are not just *homo mistakus*. If we had learned to make nothing but bad choices our species would have been consigned to the dust bin of history a long time ago, making room for some survivors less prone to error.

We clearly learned to make good choices as well, and to learn from our mistakes and even the success and wisdom of others. As I mentioned earlier, I have formally interviewed hundreds of millionaires. I am even more fascinated by choices they made that were the good (and sometimes brilliant!) ones, and the processes they used to make them.

As a human species, there is much to be admired about *homo sapiens*. We are capable of great work, soaring ideas, and wonderful compassion, all the results of good choices. And behavioral science is helping us to understand how we make those choices.

Even as what was once considered the foundations of finance (the efficient market hypothesis, CAPM, and modern portfolio theory) are being questioned and even blamed for much of the problems in the markets, many of us are looking to the new world of behavioral finance for answers to our investment conundrums. By understanding ourselves and the way we make decisions, we can often create our own systematic process for making the right choices. Whereas we once seemed to be adrift in an ocean of potential choices, with our emotions often dictating the final outcome, with the right tools we can learn to set a confident course to that safe port of call.

The problem is that behavioral finance can seem a little daunting, full of studies and inferences, and not tied together very well—until now, that is. My good friend James Montier, who literally wrote the book on behavioral finance, called *Behavioural Finance: Insights into Irrational Minds and Markets*, has now put his considerable knowledge into this small tome, *The Little Book of Behavioral Investing*.

I am no stranger to James' work. He and I worked on a lengthy chapter on behavioral finance for my book, *Bull's Eye Investing* (John Wiley & Sons). I thought I was familiar with the subject. But taking the *Little Book* on a plane ride was one of the best investments of reading time I have had in years. I found myself on all too many occasions sadly admitting to myself, "That's me!" and sighing, vowing to never again make that mistake. But at least I now know what to avoid, and I can work to improve my habits.

This is a book that I am going to have to read often, at least annually. Thankfully, James has made the book fun and the subject interesting. His naturally wry humor comes through. Whether learning why we can't seem to sell when we should, or why we choose our price targets, James gives us a blueprint to becoming better investors in 16 little chapters full of insight. No more *homo mistakus*!

I suggest you put this book on the top of your reading pile, and keep it near your desk, so you can refer to it often—to help keep you calm in the heat of the decision-making moment. So, sit back, and let James help bring out your inner Spock!

John Mauldin

Introduction

~

This Is a Book About You: You Are Your Own Worst Enemy

How could I possibly write a book about you? After all, chances are we've never met. Let alone that I know you well enough to write a book about you! The answer is actually very simple: You are a human being (unless the sales of this book have managed to reach interplanetary proportions—evidence of extreme over-optimism on my part perhaps), and we humans are all prone to stumble into mental pitfalls. This is as true in investing as it is in every other walk of life. Indeed, Ben Graham (the father of value investing) even went so far as to say "The investor's *chief* problem—and even his worst *enemy*—is likely to be himself."

Evidence of this harmful investor behavior can be found in the annual Dalbar studies, which measure the actual returns achieved by investors rather than the returns from a passive index, such as the S&P 500. They also capture the degree to which investors attempt to time their entry and exit to the market (among other things). The results aren't pretty. Over the last 20 years, the S&P 500 has generated just over 8 percent on average each year. Active managers have subtracted 1 or 2 percent from this, so you might be tempted to think that individual investors in equity funds would have earned a yearly 6 to 7 percent. However, equity fund investors have managed to reduce this to a paltry 1.9 percent per annum. This results from buying and selling at just about the worst possible point in time. Sure looks like Ben Graham was right—we really are our own worst enemies.

The goods news is that it doesn't have to be this way. We can learn to make better decisions—it isn't easy, but it is possible. *The Little Book of Behavioral Investing* will take you on a guided tour of the most common behavioral challenges and mental pitfalls that investors encounter and provide you with strategies to eliminate these innate traits. Along the way, we'll see how some of the world's best investors have tackled the behavioral biases that drag down investment returns, so that you hopefully will be able to learn from their experiences and go on to make superior returns and have fewer losses.

The Most Important Lesson of All

Whenever I teach behavioral psychology I see the audience recognizing the mental mistakes that I am talking about. However, most of the time they recognize the mistake in others, rather than in themselves. It is always Bill the trader, or Pete the portfolio manager, who illustrates the bias rather than us. We all seem to have a bias blind spot.

For instance, a group of Americans were asked to assess how likely the average American was to make a particular mental error, and how likely they themselves were to make exactly the same mistake.* The bias blind spot kicked in. The survey participants thought the average American was always more likely than they were to make a mental mistake.

However, the evidence that has been collected over the course of the last three or four decades shows that all of us are likely to encounter mental stumbling blocks at some point. So the single most important lesson I could hope to share with anyone is that the biases and mistakes we are talking about in this book are likely to affect every one of us.

Why do we all suffer these behavioral biases? The answer lies in the fact that our brains have been refined

*E. Pronin, D.Y. Lin, and L. Ross, "The Bias Blind Spot: Perceptions of Bias in Self versus Others," *Personality and Social Psychology Bulletin* 28 (2002): 369–381.

by the process of evolution, just like any other feature of our existence. But remember, evolution occurs at a glacial pace, so our brains are well designed for the environment that we faced 150,000 years ago (the African savannah) but potentially poorly suited for the industrial age of 300 years ago, and perhaps even more ill-suited for the information age in which we currently live.

As Douglas Adams, author of the sublime *Hitchhikers Guide to the Galaxy*, said, "Many were increasingly of the opinion that they'd all made a big mistake in coming down from the trees in the first place. And some said that even the trees had been a bad move, and that no one should ever have left the oceans." Leaving the trees (or perhaps the oceans) may have been our first mistake, but it certainly wasn't our last.

The Power of *Star Trek*

Psychologists have suggested that the best method of thinking about the way in which our brains work is to imagine that we have two different systems embedded within our minds. For the Trekkies out there, these two systems can, perhaps, be characterised as Dr. McCoy and Mr. Spock. McCoy was irrepressibly human, forever allowing his emotions to rule the day. In contrast, Spock (half human, half Vulcan) was determined to suppress his emotions, letting logic drive his decisions. Just in case you are the only person on this planet who has never come across *Star Trek*, the Vulcans were a humanoid species who were noted for their attempt to live by reason and logic with no interference from emotion.

The McCoy part of our brains, which we will call the X-system, is essentially the emotional approach to decision making. The X-system is actually the default option, so all information goes first to the X-system for processing. It is automatic and effortless. The judgments made by the X-system are generally based on aspects such as similarity, familiarity, and proximity (in time). These mental short-cuts allow the X-system to deal with large amounts of information simultaneously. Effectively, the X-system is a quick and dirty 'satisfying' system, which tries to give answers that are approximately (rather than precisely) correct. In order for the X-system to believe that something is valid, it may simply need to wish that it were so.

The Spock part of our brains, which we will call the C-system, is a more logical way of processing information. It requires a deliberate effort to actually engage this system. It attempts to follow a deductive, logical approach to problem solving. However, it can only handle one step at a time (like any logical process), so it is a slow and serial way of dealing with information. Evidence and logic will be required to make the C-system believe that something is true.

Of course, we all read this and think that we are Spock. However, the reality is that the X-system handles far more of our actions than we would be comfortable to admit. In fact, very often we end up trusting our initial emotional reaction, and only occasionally do we recruit the C-system to review the decision. For instance, when we stub a toe on a rock, or bang our head on a beam (an easy thing to do in my house), we curse the inanimate object despite the fact that it could not have done anything to avoid our own mistake!

Neuroscientists have found that the parts of the brain associated with the X-system are much older, evolutionarily speaking, than the parts of the brain associated with the C-system. This is to say we evolved the need for emotion before we evolved the need for logic. This might sound odd, but an example should help make the point obvious. Let's pretend that I place a glass box containing a large snake on the table in front of you. I ask you to lean forward and concentrate on the snake. If it rears up you will jump backwards (even if you aren't afraid of snakes).

The reason for this reaction is that your X-system reacted to keep you safe. In fact, a signal was generated the second your brain perceived the snake moving. The signal was sent on two different paths—a low road and a high road, if you like. The low road was part of the X-system, and sent the information straight to the amygdala (the brain's center for fear and risk). The amygdala reacts quickly, and forces the body to jump backwards.

The second part of the signal (taking the high road) sent the information on a long loop around to part of the C-system, which processes the information in a more conscious fashion, assessing the possible threat. This system points out that there is a layer of glass between you and the snake. But you have already reacted by this time. From a survival point of view, a false positive is a better response than a false negative. Emotion is designed to trump logic.

So, Are You Spock or McCoy?

Of course, we all use both systems at various points. Indeed, the evidence suggests that those with severely impaired X-systems can't make decisions at all. They end up spending all day in bed pondering the possibilities, without actually engaging in any action.

However, from an investment perspective we may well be best served by using our C-system. Lucky for us, we can test how easy it is to override the X-system. Shane Frederick of Yale (formerly of MIT) has designed a simple three-question test which is more powerful than any IQ test or SAT score at measuring the ability of the C-system to check the output of the X-system.* Together these three questions are known as the Cognitive Reflection Task (CRT).

*S. Frederick, "Cognitive Reflection and Decision Making," *Journal of Economic Perspectives* 19 (2005): 24–42.

Consider the following three questions:

1. A bat and a ball together cost $1.10 in total. The bat costs a dollar more than the ball. How much does the ball cost?
2. If it takes five minutes for five machines to make five widgets, how long would it take 100 machines to make 100 widgets?
3. In a lake there is a patch of lily pads. Every day the patch doubles in size. If it takes 48 days for the patch to cover the entire lake, how long will it take to cover half the lake?

Now each of these questions has an obvious, but unfortunately incorrect answer, and a less obvious but nonetheless correct answer. In question #1 the quick and dirty system favors an answer of $.10. However, a little logic shows that the correct answer is actually $.05.

$$1 \text{ Bat} + 1 \text{ Ball} = \$1.10$$
$$1 \text{ Bat} - 1 \text{ Ball} = \$1.00$$
$$2 \text{ Bats} = \$2.10$$
$$1 \text{ Bat} = \$1.05$$
$$\text{Therefore } 1 \text{ Ball} = \$0.05$$

In question #2 the gut reaction is often to say 100 minutes. However, with a little reflection we can see that if it takes five machines five minutes to produce five widgets, the output is actually one widget per machine per five minutes. As such, it would take 100 machines five minutes to make 100 widgets.

Finally, in question three, the most common incorrect answer is to halve the 48 days and say 24 days. However, if the patch doubles in size each day, the day before it covers the entire lake, it must have covered half the lake, so the correct answer is 47 days.

Don't worry if you got one or all three of those questions wrong—you aren't alone. In fact, after giving the test to nearly 3,500 people, Frederick found that only 17 percent of them managed to get all three questions right. Thirty-three percent got none right! The best performing group were MIT students; 48 percent of them managed to get all three questions correct—but that is still less than half of some of the best students in the world. I've had 600 professional investors (fund managers, traders, and analysts) take these questions and only 40 percent managed to get all three questions correct, while 10 percent didn't get any right.

What does this tell us? It tells us that all humans are prone to decision-making using the X-system, and this is often unchecked by the more logical C-system. I've found that the number of Frederick's questions that you get correct correlates with your general vulnerability to a whole plethora of other behavioral biases, such as loss aversion, conservatism, and impatience. Those who get zero questions right seem to suffer more pronounced examples of the biases than those who get three questions right.

Just in case you got all three questions right and are now about to abandon this book, I would caution that two very important biases seem to be immune to the power of the CRT. No matter how well you scored on the CRT you are still likely to encounter a couple of specific mental pitfalls— namely over-optimism, overconfidence, and confirmatory bias. These will be explored in the coming chapters.

X Unchecked

When are we most likely to reply upon our X-System to help us out? Psychologists* have explored this question and come up with the following conditions which increase the likelihood of X-system thinking:

- When the problem is ill structured and complex.
- When information is incomplete, ambiguous, and changing.
- When the goals are ill defined, shifting, or competing.

---

*See Gary Klein: *Sources of Power: How People Make Decisions* (Cambridge, MA: MIT Press, 1999).

- When the stress is high, because either time constraints and/or high stakes are involved.
- When decisions rely upon an interaction with others.

Now I don't know about you, but pretty much every decision of any consequence that I've ever had to make has fallen into at least one or more of those categories. It certainly characterizes many of the decisions that we make when faced with an investment proposition.

One of the world's greatest investors, Warren Buffett, has said that investors need to learn to control their X-system, "Success in investing doesn't correlate with IQ once you're above the level of 100. Once you have ordinary intelligence, what you need is the temperament to control the urges that get other people into trouble in investing."

But before we conclude that we have solved all of our behavioral errors, we should be aware that self-control (the ability to override our urges) is like a muscle—after use it needs time to recharge. To illustrate this point, think about the following experiment.*

You are told not to eat any food for the three hours prior to the exercise (actually timed so you have to skip lunch).

*M.R. Muraven and R.F. Baumeister, Self-Regulation and Depletion of Limited Resources: Does Self-Control Resemble a Muscle?" *Psychological Bulletin* 126 (2000): 247–259.

When you arrive at the lab you are put into one of three groups.

The first group is taken into a room where the aroma of freshly baked chocolate chip cookies is wafting around. This room contains two trays, one laid out with freshly baked chocolate chip cookies, the other full of radishes. The group is told they can eat as many radishes as they would like, but they mustn't eat the cookies. The second group is more fortunate. They too are faced with two trays, each containing the same foods as for the first group, but this group is told they can eat the cookies. The third group is taken to an empty room.

After 10 minutes all the groups are collected and moved to another room to take a test. The test is one of those tricky ones where you are told you must trace a shape, but do so without going over a line you have drawn before and without lifting your pen from the paper.

How do you think people from each grouped fared in the test? Those who were forced to resist the temptation of freshly baked cookies and content themselves with radishes gave up on the test in less than half the time of those from the other two groups; they also attempted just half as many problems! Their willpower had been diminished by simply resisting the temptation of cookies.

These results suggest that relying upon willpower alone is going to be tricky. Resisting the chocolate cookie that beckons to us may lead to a poor investment choice. Willpower alone is unlikely to be a sufficient defense against behavioral biases.

As Warren Buffett said, "Investing is simple but not easy." That is to say, it should be simple to understand how investing works effectively: You buy assets for less than their intrinsic value and then sell when they are trading at or above their fair value. However, the gamut of behavioral bias that we display tends to prevent us from doing what we know we should do. As Seth Klarman observes:

> So if the entire country became securities analysts, memorized Benjamin Graham's *Intelligent Investor* and regularly attended Warren Buffett's annual shareholder meetings, most people would, nevertheless, find themselves irresistibly drawn to hot initial public offerings, momentum strategies and investment fads. People would still find it tempting to day-trade and perform technical analysis of stock charts. A country of security analysts would still overreact. In short, even the best-trained investors would make the same mistakes that investors have been making forever, and for the same immutable reason—that they cannot help it.

The alternative is to ingrain better behavior into your investment approach. In the coming chapters, I will highlight some of the most destructive behavioral biases and common mental mistakes that I've seen professional investors make. I'll teach you how to recognize these mental pitfalls while exploring the underlying psychology behind the mistake. Then, I show you what you can do to try to protect your portfolio from their damaging influence on your returns. Along the way, we'll see how some of the world's best investors have striven to develop investment processes that minimize their behavioral errors.

So turn the page, and we'll start our voyage into your mind. First stop—emotions and the heat of the moment!

Chapter One

In the Heat of the Moment

~

Prepare, Plan, and Pre-Commit to a Strategy

EMOTIONAL TIME TRAVEL ISN'T OUR SPECIES' FORTE. When asked in the cold light of day how we will behave in the future, we turn out to be very bad at imagining how we will act in the heat of the moment. This inability to predict our own future behavior under emotional strain is called an empathy gap.

We all encounter empathy gaps. For instance, just after eating a large meal, you can't imagine ever being hungry again. Similarly, you should never do the supermarket shopping while hungry, as you will overbuy.

Now let's imagine you are lost in some woods. As you search though your backpack you discover that you have forgotten to bring both food and water. Oh, the horror. Which would you regret more: not bringing the food or the water?

Psychologists* have asked exactly this question of two different groups and offered them a bottle of water in return for participating. One group was asked just before they started to work out at a gym; the other group was asked immediately after a workout. If people are good emotional time travellers, the timing of the questions should have no impact at all. However, this isn't the pattern uncovered by the researchers. Sixty-one percent of the people who were asked before the workout thought they would regret not taking water more. However, after the workout, 92 percent said they would regret not taking water more!

My all-time favourite example of an empathy gap comes from an experiment by my friend Dan Ariely and his

---

*L. Van Boven and G. Loewenstein, "Projection of Transient Drive States," *Personality and Social Psychology Bulletin* 29 (2003): 1159–1168.

co-author George Loewenstein.* They asked 35 men (and it had to be men for reasons that will become all too obvious) to look at pictures of sexual stimuli on a cling-film-wrapped laptop. To save the gentle readers' blushes I have omitted the full list, but suffice it to say that acts such as spanking and bondage were included.

The subjects were asked to rate how much they would enjoy each act while in a cold state (in front of an experimenter in a classroom-like environment). The participants were then sent home and asked to reevaluate the pictures in the privacy of their own home while enjoying what might be delicately described as self-gratification.

In the cold light of day the average arousal rating was 35 percent. However, this rocketed to 52 percent when the men assessed the images in a private, aroused state. That is a massive 17 percentage point increase, driven by the heat of the moment!

The Perils of Procrastination

In order to see how we can combat empathy gaps, we must first look at the perils of procrastination—that dreadful urge you suffer, when you know there is work to be done, to put it off for as long as possible.

*Dan Ariely and George Loewenstein, "The Heat of the Moment: The Effect of Sexual Arousal on Sexual Decision Making," *Journal of Behavioral Decision Making* 19 (2006): 87–98.

Imagine you have been hired as a proofreader for a set of essays, each about 10 pages long. You have three options: You can set your own deadlines and turn in each essay separately; you can hand everything in at the last minute before a final deadline; or you can go with a predetermined set of deadlines for each essay. Which would you choose?

Most people (myself included, of course) go with handing everything in at the last moment. After all, we reason, I'll do the work at my pace and then hand it all in whenever I like.

Unfortunately, this decision ignores our tendency to procrastinate (something book editors will be all too familiar with!). While we all start off with the best of intentions to space out the work evenly, inevitably other things come up, our best-laid plans are disrupted, and we end up doing all the work at the last minute.

Yet, psychologists have found* that imposed deadlines are the most effective. Researchers split people into three groups randomly and assigned them one of the conditions outlined above. Those who were told they had to follow equally spaced deadlines found the most errors, yet handed their work in with the least delay. The group who chose their own set of deadlines found fewer errors and were nearly twice as late

*Dan Ariely and Klaus Wertenbroch, "Procrastination, Deadlines, and Performance: Self-Control by Precommitment," *Psychological Science* 13 (2002): 219–224.

handing in their reports. However, the worst-performing group was those who were allowed to wait until the final deadline to hand everything in. This group found far fewer errors than the other two groups and were nearly three times later in handing in their reports than those who worked to equally spaced deadlines. This experiment provides a possible weapon to place in our arsenal against the behavioral pitfall of empathy gaps and procrastination—pre-commitment.

The Power of Pre-Commitment

So what can we, as investors, do to prevent ourselves from falling into these emotional time travel pitfalls? One simple answer is to prepare and pre-commit. Investors should learn to follow the seven P's—: Perfect planning and preparation prevent piss poor performance. That is to say, we should do our investment research when we are in a cold, rational state—and when nothing much is happening in the markets—and then pre-commit to following our own analysis and prepared action steps.

Sir John Templeton, legendary investor and mutual fund pioneer, provides us with a perfect example of this process in action. He was well known for saying "The time of maximum pessimism is the best time to buy, and the time of maximum optimism is the best time to sell." Few would disagree with the sentiment. However, when "everyone is busy despondently selling," it can be hard to stand against the tide and buy. This difficulty is the very definition of an empathy gap.

Sir John's great-niece, Lauren C. Templeton, provides us with the strategy her uncle used to overcome this obstacle in her book, *Investing the Templeton Way*:

> There are clear psychological challenges to maintaining a clear head during a sharp sell off. One way Uncle John used to handle this was to make his buy decisions well before a sell off occurred. During his years managing the Templeton Funds, he always kept a "wish list" of securities representing companies that he believed were well run but priced too high . . . he often had standing orders with his brokers to purchase those wish list stocks if for some reason the market sold off enough to drag their prices down to levels at which he considered them a bargain.

This prime example of pre-commitment in the face of a known empathy gap is exactly what you should seek to emulate in your investment strategies. Sir John knew that on the day the market or stock was down say 40 percent he wouldn't have the discipline to execute a buy. But, by placing buy orders well below the market price, it becomes easier to buy when faced with despondent selling. This is a simple but highly effective way of removing emotion from the situation.

Chapter Two

Who's Afraid of the Big Bad Market?

Re-Investing When Terrified

LET'S PLAY A SIMPLE GAME. At the start of the game you are given $20 and told the following: The game will last 20 rounds. At the start of each round you will be asked if you would like to invest. If you say yes, the cost will be $1. A fair coin will then be flipped. If it comes up heads you will receive $2.50. If it comes up tails, you will lose your $1.

Now there are two things we know about this game. First—and perhaps most obvious—it is in your best interest to invest in all rounds due to the asymmetric nature of the payoff. That is to say, you stand to make more than you lose in each round; the expected value per round is $1.25, giving a total expected value to the game of $25. In fact, there is only a 13 percent chance that you'd end up with total earnings of less than $20, which is what you'd have if you chose not to invest at all and just kept the initial endowment. The second thing we know is that the outcome in a prior round shouldn't impact your decision to invest in the next round—after all, the coin has no memory.

However, when experimenters studied this game they found some very unusual behavior.* They asked three different groups to play the game. The first group was very unusual; they had a very specific form of brain damage—these individuals couldn't feel fear. The second group of players were people like you and me—ostensibly without any evidence of brain damage. The third group consisted of people who had brain damage but in parts of their brains unrelated to the processing of emotion (and hence fear).

Who do you think fared best? Not surprisingly, it was the group with the inability to feel fear. They invested in 84 percent of rounds, whereas the so-called normals invested

*B. Shiv, G. Loewenstein, A. Bechara, H. Damasio, and A. Damasio, "Investment Behavior and the Negative Side of Emotion," *Psychological Science* 16 (2005): 435–439.

in 58 percent of rounds, and the group with non-fear-related brain damage invested 61 percent of the time.

The group who couldn't feel fear displayed their real edge after rounds in which they had lost money. Following such rounds, they invested more than 85 percent of the time—pretty optimal behavior. This was a huge contrast with the other two groups, who displayed seriously sub-optimal behavior. In fact, so bad was the pain/fear of losing even $1 that these groups invested less than 40 percent of the time after a round in which they had suffered a loss.

You might think that, as time went on, people would learn from their mistakes and hence get better at this game. Unfortunately, the evidence suggests a very different picture. When the experimenters broke the 20 rounds down into four groups of five games, they found that those who couldn't feel fear invested a similar percentage of the time across all four groups. However, the normals started off by investing in about 70 percent of the rounds in the first five games, but ended up investing in less than 50 percent of the final five games. The longer the game went on, the worse their decision-making became.

You may be wondering why I am telling you this story—well, it naturally parallels the behaviors investors exhibit during bear markets. The evidence above suggests that fear causes people to ignore bargains when they are available in the market, especially if they have previously suffered a loss. The longer they find themselves in this position, the worse their decision-making appears to become.

Of course, this game is designed so that taking risk yields good results. If the game were reversed and taking risk ended in poor outcomes, the normals would outperform the players who can't feel fear. However, the version of the game outlined above is a good analogy to bear markets with cheap valuations, where future returns are likely to be good.

Brain Drain and Performance

A recent study* explored the same game that is outlined above, but measured people based on their degree of reliance upon X-system thinking. (For those interested in the testing format, they used a self-report approach. People were measured on the basis of how much they agreed or disagreed with eight statements, such as "I tend to use my heart as a guide for my actions," "I like to rely on my intuitive impressions," and "I don't have a very good sense of intuition," rather than a more clinical approach like the CRT that we used in Chapter 1.) It was surmised that if the depletion of mental resources such as self-control

*Bart De Langhe, Steven Sweldens, S.M.J. Van Osselaer, and Mirjam A. Tuk, "The Emotional Information Processing System Is Risk-Averse: Ego-Depletion and Investment Behavior" (Unpublished working paper, 2008).

is a problem, then those who rely more on their X-system should suffer poorer decision-making when they have been forced to use up their store of self-regulatory ability. To put it another way, those who use their quick and dirty thinking systems (X-system thinking) will run out of self-control faster than those who are more inclined to use their logical thinking systems (C-system thinking).

In order to achieve this, one group of players was subjected to a Stroop test. The Stroop test will be familiar to fans of brain training games, although they may not know its name. It presents the names of colors, and players have to name the color in which the name of the color is written, rather than the name of the color. Thus the word RED may appear in blue ink, and the correct response is blue. It thus takes concentration and willpower to complete the Stroop test.

When the game was played with a pre-test (i.e., without the Stroop test), both those who relied on X- and C-system processing performed in the same fashion. They invested about 70 percent of the time (still distinctly sub-optimally).

However, the results were very different when people were unable to control their own fear and emotions (i.e., after the Stroop test). Those with a very strong reliance on their C-system continued to do well, investing 78 percent of the time. However, those who relied heavily on their X-system suffered particularly badly. They invested only 49 percent of the time! This is yet more evidence of the dangers of relying upon our own abilities to defeat our decision-making demons.

The Cure for Temporary Paralysis

In March 2009, the S&P 500 swooned to its lowest levels in a decade, and the market had declined some 57 percent since its peak in late 2007.

I watched as markets seemed to be near meltdown. No scenario seemed to be pessimistic enough to be beyond belief among investors. How did this make me feel? Actually, very excited. Not because I have some sick perversion that means I enjoy a crisis (although I may well), but rather because markets were getting cheap. As I wrote in *Mind Matters* in early March 2009, "Buy when it's cheap—if not then, when?" The basic argument was simple enough: Markets were at levels of valuation that we simply hadn't seen for 20 to 30 years. Of course, valuation isn't a fail-safe reason for buying equities—cheap stocks can always get cheaper—but in March I was convinced that they offered a great buying opportunity for long-term investors.

I wasn't alone in thinking these thoughts. Jeremy Grantham, chief strategist of GMO, penned the following:

As this crisis climaxes, formerly reasonable people will start to predict the end of the world, armed with plenty of terrifying and accurate data that will serve to reinforce the wisdom of your caution. Every decline will enhance the beauty of cash until, as some of us experienced in 1974, "terminal paralysis" sets in. Those who were over invested will be catatonic and just sit and pray. Those few who look brilliant, oozing cash, will not want to easily give up their brilliance. So almost everyone is watching and waiting with their inertia beginning to set like concrete. Typically, those with a lot of cash will miss a very large chunk of the market recovery.

There is only one cure for terminal paralysis: you absolutely must have a battle plan for reinvestment and stick to it. Since every action must overcome paralysis, what I recommend is a few large steps, not many small ones. A single giant step at the low would be nice, but without holding a signed contract with the devil, several big moves would be safer.

It is particularly important to have a clear definition of what it will take for you to be fully invested. Without a similar program, be prepared for your committee's enthusiasm to invest (and your own for that matter) to fall with the market. You must get them to agree now—quickly before rigor mortis sets in. . . . Finally, be aware that the market does not turn when it sees light at the end of the tunnel.

It turns when all looks black, but just a subtle shade less black than the day before.

Similarly, Seth Klarman, the head of Baupost and value investor extraordinaire, wrote:

The chaos is so extreme, the panic selling so urgent, that there is almost no possibility that sellers are acting on superior information; indeed, in situation after situation, it seems clear that investment fundamentals do not factor into their decision making at all. . . . While it is always tempting to try and time the market and wait for the bottom to be reached (as if it would be obvious when it arrived), such a strategy proved over the years to be deeply flawed. Historically, little volume transacts at the bottom or on the way back up and competition from other buyers will be much greater when the markets settle down and the economy begins to recover. Moreover, the price recovery from a bottom can be very swift. Therefore, an investor should put money to work amidst the throes of a bear market, appreciating that things will likely get worse before they get better.

The advice that Grantham and Klarman so timely offered is, of course, yet another example of the power of pre-commitment that we saw in Chapter 1. The "battle plan for reinvestment" is a schedule of pre-commitments that acknowledges both the empathy gap we will likely encounter and also helps remove the fear-induced terminal paralysis that we are likely to be suffering.

While on holiday a few years ago, I asked a local for directions. His less than helpful response was, "I wouldn't start from here!" However, when it comes to investing we can actually make a difference in our starting point. As Klarman further notes, "One of our strategies for maintaining rational thinking at all times is to attempt to avoid the extreme stresses that lead to poor decision-making. We have often described our techniques for accomplishing this: willingness to hold cash in the absence of compelling investment opportunity, a strong sell discipline, significant hedging activity, and avoidance of recourse leverage, among others." By removing some of the sources of forced decisions during difficult times, Klarman attempts to reduce the vulnerability to empathy gaps and terror-driven poor decisions. Learn from his example and try to remove the drivers of forced decisions from your portfolios.

Chapter Three

Always Look on the Bright Side of Life

~

"But, Why Should I Own This Investment?"

LET ME ASK YOU THREE QUESTIONS. Don't worry, they aren't as tricky as those we encountered in the Introduction.

1. Are you above average when you drive a car?
2. Are you above average at your job?
3. Are you above average when you make love?

If you are like the vast majority of people you will have answered each of these three questions in the affirmative. Indeed, when I ask for a show of hands there is usually one gentleman who raises both hands in response to question 3 (I'm personally convinced this is extreme overconfidence, but we will leave that for the next chapter).

Optimism seems ingrained in the human psyche. At the end of Monty Python's *Life of Brian*, those hanging on crucifixes begin singing "Always look on the bright side of life." It would appear that the vast majority of people subscribe to this particular view of the world.

When I asked a sample of more than 600 professional fund managers how many of them were above average at their jobs, an impressive 74 percent responded in the affirmative. Indeed, many of them wrote comments such as, "I know everyone thinks they are, but I really am!" Similarly, some 70 percent of analysts think they are better than their peers at forecasting earnings—yet, the very same analysts had 91 percent of their recommendations as either buys or holds in February 2008. This trait is not unique to the investment industry. When teaching, I generally find that 80 percent of students believe they will finish in the top 50 percent of my class.

This tendency to overrate our abilities is amplified by the illusion of control—we think we can influence an outcome. The illusion of control crops up in some odd places.

For instance, people will pay four times more for a lottery ticket if they can pick the numbers, as opposed to a ticket with randomly selected numbers, as if the act of the person picking the numbers makes them more likely to occur.

Thus, people often mistake randomness for control. For example, when asked to predict the outcome of 30 coin tosses, which were actually rigged so that everyone guessed correctly half the time, those who got their early guesses right rated themselves as much better guessers than those who had started badly.

In fact, the illusion of control seems most likely to occur when lots of choices are available; when you have early success at the task (as per the coin tossing); the task you are undertaking is familiar to you; the amount of information is high; and you have a personal involvement. To me, these sound awfully like the conditions we encounter when investing.

Optimism and the X-System

Earlier I mentioned that even if you managed to answer all three of the cognitive reflection task questions correctly, you were still likely to be subject to several biases. Over-optimism is one of these cognitive ability resistant biases.

Optimism seems to be the default state and embedded within the X-system of processing information. We already know that the X-system is more likely to be used when a person feels pressured by time. So, if optimism is indeed part of the X-system we should be able to coax it out by putting people through their paces against the clock.

This is exactly what psychologists have done.* Participants were placed in front of a computer screen and shown statements about future life events. They could press either a key labeled "not me" or a key labeled "me." Subjects were told how commonly the events occurred in the general population. The event appeared on the screen for either 1 or 10 seconds. Six positive and six negative life events were used.

When allowed time to consider the life events, participants said that 4 of the 6 positive life events would happen to them, but only 2.7 of the negative life events would happen to them. When placed under time pressure, the number of positive life events rose to 4.75, while the number of negative life events fell to 2.4. This pattern is consistent with the idea that optimism is a default response.

Further evidence of the deep-seated nature of our optimism is found in recent work by neuroscientists.† They have been busy scanning people's brains while asking them

---

*Heather C. Lench and Peter H. Ditto, "Automatic Optimism: Biased Use of Base Rate Information for Positive and Negative Events," *Journal of Experimental Social Psychology* 44 (2008): 631–639.

†Tali Sharot, A.M. Riccardi, C.M. Raio, and E.A. Phelps, "Neural Mechanisms Mediating Optimism Bias," *Nature* 450 (2009): 102–105.

to consider both good and bad events in their past and future. When imagining positive future events (relative to negative ones) two key areas of the brain showed increased activation: the rostral anterior cingulated cortex and the amygdala. Both of these areas are associated with emotional processing and are generally held to be neural correlates of the X-system.

Nature versus Nurture

Effectively the sources of optimism can be split into those related to nature and those related to nurture. So let's start with nature. Many of the biases we have today presumably had some evolutionary advantage (although some may be spandrels, to borrow Stephen Jay Gould's expression for the by-products of evolution).

What possible role could optimism have played in our evolution as a species? Lionel Tiger argued in his book *Optimism: The Biology of Hope* (1979) that when early man left the forests and became hunters many of them suffered injury and death. Tiger suggests that humans tend to abandon tasks associated with negative consequences, so it was biologically adaptive for humans to develop a sense of optimism. After all, it must have needed a great deal of courage to take on a mastodon (a very large prehistoric elephant-like creature); frankly, not too many pessimists would even bother.

Tiger also argues that when we are injured, our bodies release endorphins. Endorphins generally have two properties; they have an analgesic property (to reduce pain) and they produce feelings of euphoria. Tiger suggests that it was biologically adaptive for our ancestors to experience positive emotions instead of negative emotions when they were injured because it would reinforce their tendency to hunt in the future.

Optimism may also endow us with some other benefits. Psychologists have found that optimists seem to cope far better (and survive much longer) when faced with dire news over illness or other problems than pessimists do.* So optimism may well be a great *life* strategy. However, hope isn't a good *investment* strategy.

Ben Graham was well aware of the dangers of over-optimism. He noted:

Observation over many years has taught us that the chief losses to investors come from the purchase of *low-quality* securities at times of favorable business conditions. The purchasers view the current good earnings as equivalent to "earning power" and assume that prosperity is synonymous with safety.

*S.E. Taylor and J. Brown, "Illusion and Well-Being: A Social Psychological Perspective on Mental Health," *Psychological Bulletin* 103 (1988): 193–210.

So much for nature. Nurture also helps to generate the generally rose-tinted view of life. Psychologists have often documented a "self-serving bias" whereby people are prone to act in ways that are supportive of their own interests. But, as Warren Buffett warns, "Never ask a barber if you need a haircut."

Auditors provide a good example of this bias. One hundred thirty-nine professional auditors were given five different auditing cases to examine.* The cases concerned a variety of controversial aspects of accounting. For instance, one covered the recognition of intangibles, one covered revenue recognition, and one concerned capitalization versus expensing of expenditures. The auditors were told the cases were independent of each other.

The auditors were randomly assigned to either work for the company or work for an outside investor who was considering investing in the company in question. The auditors who were told they were working for the company were 31 percent more likely to accept the various dubious accounting moves than those who were told they worked for the outside investor. So much for an impartial outsider—and this was in the post-Enron age!

*Don A. Moore, George Loewenstrin, Lloyd Tanyu, and Max H. Bazerman, "Auditor Independence, Conflict of Interest and Unconscious Intrusion of Bias" (Unpublished paper, 2004).

We see this kind of self-serving bias rear its head regularly when it comes to investing. For instance, stockbroker research generally conforms to three self-serving principles:

Rule 1: All news is good news (if the news is bad, it can always get better).

Rule 2: Everything is always cheap (even if you have to make up new valuation methodologies).

Rule 3: Assertion trumps evidence (never let the facts get in the way of a good story).

Remembering that these rules govern much of what passes for research on Wall Street can help protect you from falling victim to this aspect of self-serving bias.

The most recent financial crisis provides plenty of examples of self-serving bias at work, the most egregious of which is the behavior of the ratings agencies. They pretty much perjured themselves in pursuit of profit. The conflicts of interest within such organizations are clear; after all, it is the issuer who pays for the rating, which, as with the auditors above, makes the ratings agency predisposed to favoring them. In the housing crisis, they seemed to adopt some deeply flawed quant models which even cursory reflection should have revealed were dangerous to use. But use them they did, and so a lot of sub-investment grade loans were suddenly transformed, as if by financial alchemy, into AAA rated securities.

Beating Over-Optimism

What can we do to defend ourselves against over-optimism? We must learn to think critically and become more skeptical. We should get used to asking "Must I believe this?" rather than the far more common "Can I believe this?" As the philosopher George Santayana wrote "Skepticism is the chastity of the intellect, and it is shameful to surrender it too soon or to the first comer." These words hold as true in investing as they do in life generally.

Indeed, most of the best investors appear to ask themselves a very different default question from the rest of us. Many of these investors generally run concentrated portfolios, with the default question being "Why should I own this investment?" Whereas for fund managers who are obsessed with tracking error and career risk, the default question changes to "Why shouldn't I own this stock?" This subtle distinction in default questions can have a dramatic impact upon performance.

Spencer Davidson of General American Investors recalls, "An early mentor of mine started out during the Depression and used to always say we were in the rejection business—that we're paid to be cynical and that a big part of success in investing is knowing how to say no."

Before we leave the topic of over-optimism, it is worth noting that one group of people actually see the world the way it really is—the clinically depressed! They have no illusions about their own abilities. It is this realistic viewpoint that tends to lead them to depression.

For instance, when put in a room with a light which comes on 75 percent of the time that you touch the switch, and 75 percent of the time when you don't touch the switch, most people come out saying that they have a high level of control over the light. However, the clinically depressed come out and say they had virtually no control over the light.*

Perhaps this leaves investors with an unenviable choice; either be depressed and see the world the way it is or be happy and deluded. Personally, I guess the best solution may be to be clinically depressed at work, but happy and deluded when you go home (well, it works for me anyway!).

---

*L.B. Alloy and L.Y. Abramson, "Judgments of Contingency in Depressed and Non-Depressed Students: Sadder but Wiser?," *Journal of Experimental Psychology* 108 (1979): 441–485.

Chapter Four

Why Does Anyone Listen to These Guys?

Stop Listening to the Experts!

OKAY, IT IS POP QUIZ TIME AGAIN.

Following are 10 questions. I'd like you to give a high and a low estimate for each question. Make sure that you are 90 percent sure the high and low estimates you give will surround the actual answer. (The answers can be found in the note at the bottom of page 56.)

	90% Confidence Range	
	Low	High
Martin Luther King's age at death		
Length of the Nile River (in miles)		
Number of countries in OPEC		
Number of books in the Old Testament		
Diameter of the moon (in miles)		
Weight of an empty Boeing 747 (in pounds)		
Year of Wolfgang Amadeus Mozart's birth		
Gestation period of an Asian elephant (in days)		
Air distance from London to Tokyo (in miles)		
Deepest known point in the ocean (in feet)		

If you are like most people you'll find that somewhere between four and seven of your range answers will not include the correct answer. The simple reason is that we are generally far too confident in our abilities. But, what's more shocking—or more detrimental to our portfolios—is that experts are even worse!

One of the most supported findings in psychology is that experts are generally even more overconfident than the rest of us. Don't believe me: Let's look at two groups of experts, weathermen and doctors. Each group is given information relative to their own discipline—weathermen are given weather patterns and asked to predict the weather, and doctors are given case notes and asked to diagnose the patient. They are also asked how confident they are in their predictions.

Contrary to popular belief, the weathermen were surprisingly good at this. When they think they are going to be right half the time, they are indeed right half the time. In contrast, doctors turn out to be a terrifying bunch of people. When they think they will be right 90 percent of the time they are actually correct only 15 percent of the time.

Why the difference between these two groups? In part, the difference stems from the degree of feedback each group receives. The weathermen know they are pretty hopeless forecasters, and therefore have enormously wide confidence intervals. For instance, if you are in the United Kingdom and you listen to a weather forecast it will go along these lines: There is a small chance of a sunny spell, a large probability of scattered showers, a possibility of some snow on the highlands, and the outside chance of a typhoon in the Channel. Of course, they effectively covered all possible outcomes. Weathermen can also take a peek outside and see if they are being even vaguely accurate in their forecast.

In contrast, doctors tend not to receive good feedback. In addition, our species has an unfortunate habit of using confidence as a proxy for skill. If you go to a doctor and say, "Doctor, I've got this dreadful rash," and the doctor responds, "Don't worry, I know exactly what that is. Take these tablets and you'll be fine in a week," the chances are you come away happy and reassured.

Now let's imagine you live in an alternative reality. You walk into the doctor's office and say, "Doctor, I've got this dreadful rash," and the doctor responds, "Good God, yes, that is horrible. I've never seen anything like this before. Do you think it might be contagious? Try taking these pills and if you are alive in a week come back and see me." Chances are you aren't going to feel very happy about the whole experience.

Why Does Anyone Listen to Jim Cramer?

We want people to sound confident. In fact, we love people to sound confident. Psychologists have repeatedly found that people prefer those who sound confident and are even willing to pay more for confident (but inaccurate) advisors.* I guess that explains why people listen to Jim Cramer!

For instance, in one experiment volunteers were given cash for correctly guessing the weight of people from their photographs.† In each round, the guessers bought advice from one of four volunteer advisors. The guessers could see in advance how confident each of these advisors was.

*P.C. Price and E.R. Stone, "Intuitive Evaluation of Likelihood Judgment Producers: Evidence for a Confidence Heuristic," *Journal of Behavioral Decision Making* 17 (2004): 39–57.
†J.R. Radzevick and D.A. Moore, "Competing to Be Certain (but Wrong): Social Pressure and Overprecision in Judgment" (Working paper, 2009).

Right from the outset, the more confident advisors found more buyers for their advice. This caused our friend from the previous chapter—self-serving bias—to rear its ugly head as the advisors responded by giving answers that were more and more precise as the game progressed. This effect appears to be purely a function of the market. When guessers simply had to choose whether or not to buy advice from a single advisor, the escalation of precision vanished.

You might think that the guessers would learn to avoid the overconfident advisors. The good news is that the longer the game was played, the more the guessers tended to avoid advisors who had been wrong previously. Unfortunately, this good sense was significantly outweighed by the bias towards confidence. As long as you were wrong but sounded extremely confident, even a poor track record was excused. Such is the power of confidence.

Not only do we like our experts to sound confident, but our brain actually switches off some of our natural defenses when we are told someone is an expert. Neuroscientists have recorded subjects' brain activity with an MRI machine while they made simulated financial decisions.*

*J.B. Engelmann, C.M. Capra, C. Noussair, and G.S. Berns, "Expert Financial Advice Neurobiologically 'Offloads' Financial Decision-Making under Risk" (2009): PLoS ONE 4(3): 4957.doi:10.1371/journal. pone.0004957.

During each test round, subjects had to choose between receiving a risk-free payment and trying their chances at a lottery. In some rounds they were presented with advice from an "expert economist" as to which alternative they considered to be better.

The results are worrying. Expert advice attenuated activity in areas of the brain that correlate with valuation and probability weighting. In other words, the experts' advice made the brain switch off some processes required for financial decision-making. The players' behavior simply echoed the experts' advice. Unfortunately, the expert advice given in the experiment was suboptimal—meaning the subjects could have done better had they weighed their options themselves. Beware of experts!

The Shocking Dangers of Doing What We Are Told

There is one other reason why we should be especially leery of experts—they are authority figures. By virtue of being an expert we endow them as authorities in their fields, and unfortunately we tend to blindly follow authority.

For many years I had a sign next to my desk that said "Don't question authority. They don't know the answer either!" This rather sums up my general disregard for authority. However, not many seem to share my distaste.

The classic work on obedience to authority is Stanley Milgram's experiments from the 1960s. Milgram was fascinated by questions such as why so many ordinary people followed the clearly abhorrent policies of their leaders during World War II.

Milgram devised a simple but stunningly effective experiment to illustrate our blind obedience to authority. Subjects were told they would be administering electric shocks to a "learner" at the instruction of a "teacher." The subjects were told they were involved in a study of punishment effects on learning and memory.

Those taking part sat in front of a box with electric switches on it. The switches displayed the level of voltage that was being delivered, and a text description of the level of pain ranging from "slight" through to "extreme intensity shock," to "Danger: severe shock," and culminating in "XXX." When the switches were depressed, a buzzing sound could be heard. The person playing the role of the teacher wore a white lab coat, carried a clipboard, and instructed the subjects when to press the button.

In the classic variant of this experiment, the subjects couldn't see the person they were shocking (although they did meet them at the start of the experiment), but they could hear them. At 75 volts, the learner would grunt; at 120 volts the learner started to verbally complain, warning that he had a heart condition; at 150 volts he demanded to be released; at 285 volts the learner made a noise that Milgram said could only be described as "an agonized scream." Thereafter the subject could only hear silence in response to further administered shocks.

When this experiment is described, people believe that they would stop very early in the process. Indeed, a panel of 40 psychiatrists asked by Milgram thought that only 1 percent of people would be willing to administer the maximum shock level. After all, they reasoned, Americans just don't engage in such behavior.

However, the psychiatrists were in for a hard dose of reality. One hundred percent of ordinary Americans were willing to send up to 135 volts (at which point the learner is asking to be released) through someone they didn't know. Eighty percent were willing to go up to 285 volts (at which point they were hearing screams of agony). More than 62 percent of subjects were willing to administer the maximum 450 volts, despite the machine label warnings of severe danger and "XXX."

Milgram ran many different variants of his experiments in order to understand the conditions that influence the likelihood of people's obedience to authority. The highest compliance rate was found when the subjects were not asked to administer the shock themselves; instead another confederate of the experimenter was employed as a second subject. The true subject was asked to read out the questions.

So at any time, the subjects could have objected to the experiment, walked out, or even stopped the other subject from administering the shock. However, a truly terrifying 93 percent of people sat and watched somebody reach the maximum voltage. Providing some distance from the actual implementation seemed to markedly increase compliance to authority.

Milgram's shocking experiments (if you excuse the pun) highlight the mindless way in which we follow authority. When investing, we need to learn to be far more skeptical of experts and their authority.

Fund Managers: Weathermen or Doctors?

Okay, enough of the depressing reality of our sheep-like nature for now (more later, I promise). It is time to turn our attention once again to fund managers. It might be tempting to think that fund managers are more akin to weathermen, but sadly the evidence suggests that investment professionals are the one group of people who make doctors look like they know what they are doing.

In one study, professional investors were pitted against students in a psychology course.* All the participants were asked to select one stock from a pair as being likely

---

*G. Torngren and H. Montgomery, "Worse Than Chance? Performance and Confidence among Professionals and Laypeople in the Stock Market," *Journal of Behavioral Finance* 5 (2004): 3.

to outperform the other every month. All the companies were well-known blue-chip names, and players were given the name, industry, and prior 12 months' performance for each stock.

Overall, the students were around 59 percent confident in their stock-picking skills. The professionals were on average 65 percent confident of their abilities. Sadly, you would have been better off flipping a coin than listening to either group. The students picked the right stock 49 percent of the time, while the professionals picked the right stock less than 40 percent of the time. When the professionals said they were 100 percent confident in their picks, that is to say there was no doubt in their mind that they had picked the right stock, they were actually right less than 12 percent of the time!

What was behind this appalling performance? Well, the players were asked to rank the factors they relied upon in reaching their decisions. The students said that guessing was their primary input (as was to be expected). The single biggest factor in the professionals' decisions was "other knowledge"—things that the experts thought they knew about the stocks in question from outside the scope of the study. This is a clear example of the illusion of knowledge driving overconfidence (more on this in Chapter 5).

Overconfidence May Be Hazardous to Your Wealth

What happens when overconfidence meets the market? Of course, in classical economics no one is overconfident. In fact, stock markets shouldn't even really exist in the most extreme form of efficient market theory. Why? If the price is right (as it must be under efficient markets), then why would anyone want to trade, so volumes should be zero.

As soon as you add overconfidence into one of these models, volumes and turnover explode because everyone thinks they know more than everyone else, and hence they trade more. Terry Odean and Brad Barber have explored the impact that overconfidence has on performance.*

They looked at 66,000 accounts from a discount brokerage over the period 1991–1996. The market returned just under 18 percent per annum over this time. Those individuals who traded most frequently (with a monthly turnover rate of 21.5 percent) averaged net (after fees) returns of less than 12 percent per annum. Those with

*Terrance Odean and Brad Barber, "Trading Is Hazardous to Your Wealth: The Common Stock Investment Performance of Individual Investors," *Journal of Finance* LV (2000): 773–806.

the lowest turnover managed to earn almost 18 percent per annum (after fees). Any informational advantage that high turnover individuals had was more than eradicated by the costs of trading.

One group has been found to be more over-optimistic and more over-confident than every other group in psychology studies—sadly for me, it is men. Terry and Brad also wanted to see if this showed up in trading behavior.* It did. Women had markedly lower annual turnover rates, 53 percent, compared to men's 77 percent. Women ended up with higher net returns than men.

As if this weren't bad enough, Terry and Brad also examined the performance of a group of accounts where you need your spouse's permission to trade. Those men who needed their wives' permission to trade outperformed the single guys. Unfortunately, those women who needed their husband's permission to trade underperformed the single women. So not only are men bad traders, they are a bad influence as well.

When I present these findings to the professionals they are all too happy to laugh at the misfortune of the individual investor. Yet they themselves are hardly immune

---

*Brad Barber and Terrance Odean, "Boys Will Be Boys: Gender, Overconfidence, and Common Stock Investment," *Quarterly Journal of Economics* 116 (2001): 261–292.

to overconfidence's insidious ways. Perhaps the most striking example of overconfidence among professionals is their general belief that they can outsmart everyone else—effectively, get in before everyone else and get out before the herd dashes for the exit. This is not a new phenomenon. None other than the great John Maynard Keynes wrote the following lines in 1936:

> Professional investment may be likened to those newspaper competitions in which the competitors have to pick out the six prettiest faces from a hundred photographs, the prize being awarded to the competitor whose choice most nearly corresponds to the average preferences of the competitors as a whole; so that each competitor has to pick, not those faces which he himself finds prettiest, but those which he thinks likeliest to catch the fancy of the other competitors, all of whom are looking at the problem from the same point of view. It is not a case of choosing those which, to the best of one's judgment, are really the prettiest, nor even those which average opinion genuinely thinks the prettiest. We have reached the third degree where we devote our intelligences to anticipating what average opinion expects the average opinion to be. And there are some, I believe, who practice the fourth, fifth, and higher degrees.

EXHIBIT 4.1   Keynes' Beauty Contest: The Professionals' Results

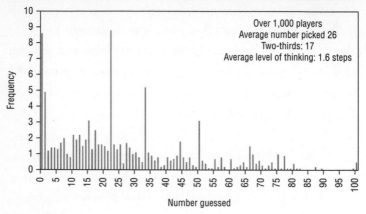

Source: GMO.

This game can be easily replicated by asking people to pick a number between 0 and 100, and telling them the winner will be the person who picks the number closest to two-thirds of the average number picked. Exhibit 4.1 shows the results from the largest game that I have played—in fact the third largest game ever played, and the only one played purely among professional investors.

The highest possible correct answer is 67. To go for 67 you have to believe that every other muppet in the known universe has just gone for 100. The fact that we got a whole raft of responses above 67 is more than slightly alarming.

In Exhibit 4.1, you can see spikes that represent various levels of thinking. The spike at 50 reflects what we (somewhat rudely) call level zero thinkers. They are the investment equivalent of Homer Simpson, 0, 100, duh 50. Not a vast amount of cognitive effort expended here!

There is a spike at 33 from those who expect everyone else in the world to be Homer. There's a spike at 22, again those who obviously think everyone else is at 33. As you can see there is also a spike at zero. Here we find all the economists, game theorists, and mathematicians of the world—clearly they have no friends. They are the only people trained to solve these problems backwards. And indeed the only stable Nash equilibrium is zero (two-thirds of zero is still zero). However, it is only the "correct" answer when everyone chooses zero.

The final noticeable spike is at 1. These contestants are economists who have (mistakenly) been invited to one dinner party (economists never get invited to more than one dinner party). They have gone out into the world and realized the rest of the world doesn't think like them. So they try to estimate the scale of irrationality. However, they end up suffering the curse of knowledge—once you know the true answer, you tend to anchor to it. In this game, which is fairly typical, the average number picked was 26, giving a two-thirds average of 17. Yet, just three people out of more than 1,000 picked the number 17.

I play this game to try to illustrate how hard it is to be just one step ahead of everyone else, to get in before everyone else, and to get out before everyone else. Yet despite this fact, it seems that this is exactly what a large number of investors spend their time doing—trying to be the smartest person in the room.

So if we can't outsmart everyone else, how on earth can we invest? The good news is that we don't need to outsmart everyone else. We need to stick to our investment discipline, ignore the actions of others, and stop listening to the so-called experts.

So, the next time a financial talking head tries to talk you into anything, do yourself a favor, put your fingers in your ears, and start humming to yourself!

Answers to pop quiz: 39 years; 4,187 miles; 13 countries; 39 books; 2,160 miles; 390,000 lbs; 1756; 645 days; 5,959 miles; 36,198 ft.

Chapter Five

The Folly of Forecasting

Prepare—Don't Predict

As the sixth-century BC poet and philosopher Lao Tzu observed, "Those who have knowledge don't predict. Those who predict don't have knowledge." Yet, most of the investment industry seems to be obsessed with trying to guess the future. This stems from the way many investors are taught to think about investing. For instance, when we learn about the favorite valuation metric of finance—discounted cash flow—we are taught that we have to forecast cash flows for the firm way into the future, and then discount them back to the present.

However, as Charlie Munger has pointed out, "Some of the worst business decisions I've ever seen are those with future projections and discounts back. It seems like the higher mathematics with more false precision should help you but it doesn't. They teach that in business schools because, well, they've got to do something."

This whole enterprise of trying to be a financial soothsayer seems largely doomed to failure because of the behavior pitfall from the previous chapter—overconfidence.

Let's say you invest according to the following process: Forecast the economy, forecast the path of interest rates, forecast the sectors which will do well within that environment, and finally forecast which stocks will do well within that sector.

Now let's assume you are pretty good at this and you are right on each forecast 70 percent of the time, which is massively above the actual rates of accuracy that we generally see. If you require all four forecasts to be correct, then you have just a 24 percent chance of actually getting it right. (This assumes that each of the forecasts is an independent event.) Now think about the number of forecasts an average analyst's model contains—sales, costs, margins, taxes, and so on. No wonder these guys are never right.

In addition, even if by some miracle of divine intervention your forecast turns out to be correct, you can only make money from it, if (and only if) it is different from the consensus. This adds a whole new dimension of complexity to the problem.

The evidence on the folly of forecasting is overwhelming and would fill many Little Books in its own right. So, let's just skate through a few facts and figures to give you a gist of the problem.

We'll start at the top with the economists. These guys haven't got a clue. Frankly, the three blind mice have more credibility at seeing what is coming than any macro-forecaster. For instance, the consensus of economists has completely failed to predict any of the last four recessions (even once we were in them).

The analysts are no better. Their forecasting record is simply dreadful on both short- and long-term issues. When an analyst first makes a forecast for a company's earnings two years prior to the actual event, they are on average wrong by a staggering 94 percent. Even at a 12-month time horizon, they are wrong by around 45 percent! To put it mildly, analysts don't have a clue about future earnings.

Their performance in divining the longer-term future is no better than their nonexistent ability to forecast the short term. When looking at the five-year growth rate forecasts from analysts versus the actual outcomes, a rather depressing reality asserts itself. The stocks that analysts expect to grow the fastest actually grow no faster than the stocks they expect to grow the slowest! Of course, buying the stocks that they expect to grow the fastest just means signing up for massive disappointment. For now we can content ourselves by saying that analysts have absolutely no idea about forecasting long-term growth.

Analysts also have an embarrassing track record when it comes to target prices. As Ben Graham said, "Forecasting security prices is not properly a part of security analysis," but that doesn't stop the analysts from coming up with daft guesses as to the future price of a stock. On average these targets are about 25 percent higher than the current price. However, they are worthless as forecasts. For instance, in 2000 the average target price of stocks was some 37 percent above the market price at the start of the year. The actual outcome was that they were up 16 percent. In 2008, the analysts forecasted a 24 percent price *increase*, yet stocks actually *fell* nearly 40 percent. In fact, between 2000 and 2008, the analysts hadn't even managed to get the direction of change in prices right in four out of nine years.

The bottom line from this whistle stop tour of the failure of forecasting is that it would be sheer madness to base an investment process around our seriously flawed ability to divine the future. We would all be better off if we took Keynes' suggested response when asked about the future, "We simply do not know."

So, Why Do We Keep Forecasting?

If forecasts are really so bad, the natural question becomes: Why do people keep producing them? In part it is a case of demand creating supply. If investors want such meaningless information, then someone will provide it to them. I've had countless discussions with both analysts and their managers over the years as to the total pointlessness of issuing target prices; their last line of defense is always "The clients want them."

Yet, one might wonder if forecasters eventually get bored with being utterly wrong and would like to give up guessing the future. However, experts seem to use a variety of excuses for forecast failure that allow them to avoid admitting they can't forecast.

Philip Tetlock has done one of the most comprehensive studies of forecasters, their accuracy, and their excuses. When studying experts' views on a wide range of world political events over a decade, he found that, across the vast array of predictions, experts who reported they had 80 percent or more confidence in their predictions were actually correct only around 45 percent of the time.* Across all predictions, the experts were little better than coin tossers.

After each of the events passed, the forecasts were shown to be either right or wrong. Tetlock returned to the experts and asked them to reassess how well they thought they understood the underlying process and forces at work. Despite the incontrovertible evidence that they were wrong, the experts showed no sign of cutting their faith in their own understanding of the situation.

Instead of any self-insight, Tetlock uncovered five frequently used excuses as to why the experts' forecasts were wrong (which reminds me of the old description of an economist being an expert who will know tomorrow why the things he predicted yesterday didn't happen today).

The most common excuses were:

1. The "If only" defense—If only the Federal Reserve had raised rates, then the prediction would have been true. Effectively, the experts claim that they would have been correct if only their advice had been followed.

*Philip Tetlock, "Theory-Driven Reasoning about Plausible Pasts and Probable Futures in World Politics," in *Heuristics and Biases: The Psychology of Intuitive Judgement,* ed. T. Gilovich, D. Griffen, and D. Kahneman (Cambridge University Press, 2003).

2. The "*ceteris paribus*" defense—Something outside of the model of analysis occurred, which invalidated the forecast; therefore it isn't my fault.

3. The "I was almost right" defense—Although the predicted outcome didn't occur, it almost did.

4. The "It just hasn't happened yet" defense—I wasn't wrong, it just hasn't occurred yet. This is my personal favorite.

5. The "Single prediction" defense—You can't judge me by the performance of a single forecast.

These excuses allowed the failed forecasters to continue making outrageously poor forecasts without any acknowledgment that they really got it wrong.

Despite coming from a very different arena (politics), the list of excuses outlined above can also be found frequently in of the word of investing. Two psychologists* explored the excuses produced by financial analysts (extremely overconfident, as we saw in the last chapter) and by weathermen (well calibrated in the last chapter), when they got it wrong. The weathermen were disarmingly honest in explaining their errors. The most frequently cited reason for their failure was "personal inexperience,"

*T. Tyska and P. Zielonka, "Expert Judgments: Financial Analysts versus Weather Forecasters," *Journal of Psychology and Financial Markets* 3 (2002): 152–160.

followed by an acknowledgment that they were trying to forecast the inherently unforecastable.

Strangely enough, a very different set of excuses was encountered when it came to the financial analysts. Their most common defense was that they shouldn't be judged on the basis of just one forecast, which is known as the single prediction defense, followed by the excuse that something else happened outside of the scope of their model, which is the *ceteris paribus* defense. So next time you hear an expert trotting out an excuse to explain why they didn't predict what actually happened, you can listen and see which of these paltry defenses they deploy, but I suggest that you just run—not walk—away.

Why Do We Use Forecasts?

We now have some idea of why it is that people continue to produce forecasts, even if they are useless. However, we are still left with the bigger question: Why do people keep blindly following these useless forecasts?

As we stated at the outset of this chapter, we have all been taught that we need forecasts to help us invest. This viewpoint was typified in an article that Joe Nocera wrote for the *New York Times* on October 1, 2005, in which he opined:

> Indeed, I wound up thinking that forecasting is to the market what gravity is to the earth. As much as

we like to poke fun at faulty predictions, we can't function without them. Even if we disagree with, say, the analysts' consensus on Cisco, that consensus gives us a basis that helps us to form our own judgments about whether it is overvalued or undervalued. Without forecasts, the market would no longer be grounded to anything.

Now, I doubt that we do actually need forecasts to help us invest. But Nocera inadvertently points us to one of the reasons why people keep using forecasts: When given a number we tend to cling to it, even subconsciously—a trait known as anchoring.

For instance, I've asked 600 fund managers to write down the last four digits of their telephone numbers, and then to estimate the number of physicians that work in London. Oddly, those with telephone numbers of 7,000 or higher think there are around 8,000 doctors working in London, while those with telephone numbers of 3,000 or lower think there are around 4,000 doctors in London. I haven't got a clue as to how many doctors there are in London, but I am sure that my best guess would be unrelated to my telephone number!

Others have shown that legal experts were influenced by irrelevant anchors when setting jail sentences, even when the experts were fully aware of the irrelevance of the input.*

In one study, participants (judges) were asked to roll dice to determine the sentencing request from the prosecution. The pair of dice they used was loaded to give either a low number (1, 2) or a high number (3, 6). Having rolled the dice, participants were told to sum the scores and this number represented the prosecution's demand. Since the judges themselves rolled the dice, they could clearly see that the input was totally irrelevant. However, the group who received the total score of 3 issued an average sentence of 5.3 months; those who received a total score of 9 issued an average sentence of 7.8 months! So, even by providing a clearly spurious forecast, people are likely to cling to it.

As an aside, think about the danger that this problem poses when it comes to so-called modern risk management. Just giving someone a measure such as value-at-risk means that they will start to hang onto it, even if they are aware that such measures are deeply flawed. But, alas, this topic is outside the scope of this Little Book; however, if you would like more information about the madness

---

*B. Englich, T. Mussweiler, and F. Strack, "Playing Dice with Criminal Sentences: The Influence of Irrelevant Anchors on Experts' Judicial Decision Making," *Personality and Social Psychology Bulletin* 32 (2006): 188–200.

of modern risk management, I suggest you consult my previous book, *Value Investing*.

There's Got to Be a Better Way

So, if we can't invest by forecasting, how should we invest? As Ben Graham pointed out "Analysis should be penetrating not prophetic." That is to say, analysts are called analysts, not forecasters, for a reason. All investors should devote themselves to understanding the nature of the business and its intrinsic worth, rather than wasting their time trying to guess the unknowable future.

Different investors have approached the problem of forecasting in different ways. If you are wedded to the use of discounted cash flow valuations, then you may well benefit from turning the process on its head. Rather than trying to forecast the future, why not take the current market price and back out what it implies for future growth. This implied growth can then be matched against a distribution of the growth rates that all firms have managed to achieve over time. If you find yourself with a firm that is at the very limits of what previous firms have achieved, then you should think very carefully about your purchase.

For instance, in January 2008, I ran a reverse engineered DCF model of the sort I've just discussed, which showed that Google, Apple, and RIMM were all pricing in 40 percent per annum growth each and every year for the next 10 years. Comparing this with a historical distribution of the 10-year growth rates achieved by all firms over a long period showed that the very best of the best (the 99.99 percentile) had only managed to grow at 22 percent per annum over 10 years. So, the market was saying that these firms would not only do better than almost any firm that ever existed, but they would double the previous record. This struck me as exceedingly unlikely. Indeed, those three stocks lost 53, 52, and 65 percent respectively over the course of 2008.

This approach harnesses the power of the outside view (i.e., the statistical evidence) to offset the inside view (i.e., our own personal viewpoint). Daniel Kahneman, the pioneer of the behavioral approach, relates a wonderful story that shows the power of the inside view. He and a group of colleagues were involved in setting up a new curriculum to teach judgment and decision-making to high school kids. After about a year, the group had written a couple of chapters for the textbook and had some outlines for sample classes. The question arose as to how long it would take to finish the project. Kahneman asked each participant to independently estimate the time to completion, and he then averaged the outcomes. He found that the estimates all clustered around 2 years, and all the estimates were between 18 and 30 months.

Since one of his colleagues was particularly experienced at this kind of activity, Kahneman asked him to think about his past experiences and what they might suggest. This experienced member replied sheepishly that 40 percent of the groups he had worked with on similar projects had never managed to finish the task, and that none of the groups had completed in less than seven years! This is the power of the outside view. When applied properly you can harness evidence to help assess the underlying odds.

An alternative approach has been pioneered by Bruce Greenwald at Columbia University. Bruce's approach compares asset value—a Ben Graham-like concept that essentially looks at the value of a firm if it were to go bust—to earnings power value, a measure of normalized earnings. Bruce then evaluates the difference between the valuations against the competitive environment, providing him with an outlook for future profits and intrinsic value. Since this is a *Little Book* I don't have the space to go into greater depth, but interested readers could do no better than seeking out Greenwald's marvellous book.*

One final approach with which I have much sympathy is best represented by Howard Marks of Oaktree Capital.

---

*Bruce Greenwald, J. Kahn, P. Sonkin, and M. Van Biema, *Value Investing: From Graham to Buffett and Beyond* (New York: John Wiley & Sons, 2001).

As he succinctly puts it, "You can't predict, you can prepare." Marks shares my scepticism towards the use of forecasts. In a memo written to Oaktree's clients in November 2001 he wrote:

> There are a few things I dismiss and a few I believe in thoroughly. The former include economic forecasts, which I think don't add value, and the list of the latter starts with cycles and the need to prepare for them.
>
> "Hey," you might say, "that's contradictory. The best way to prepare for cycles is to predict them, and you just said it can't be done." That's absolutely true, but in my opinion by no means debilitating. All of investing consists of dealing with the future . . . and the future is something we can't know much about. But the limits on our foreknowledge needn't doom us to failure as long as we acknowledge them and act accordingly.
>
> In my opinion, the key to dealing with the future lies in knowing where you are, even if you can't know precisely where you're going. Knowing where you are in a cycle and what that implies for the future is different from predicting the timing, extent and shape of the cyclical move.

This echoes Ben Graham's words that you don't need to know a person's exact weight to know whether they are overweight or underweight.

None of the three approaches goes anywhere near a forecast. Yet each has proven investment merit. Of course, this will be anathema to at least 80 percent of those working in or teaching finance and investment. The idea of investing without pretending you know the future gives you a very different perspective, and once you reject forecasting for the waste of time that it is, you will free up your time to concentrate on the things that really matter. So, when trying to overcome this behavioral pitfall, remember what Keynes said, "I'd prefer to be approximately right rather than precisely wrong."

Chapter Six

Information Overload

~

*Distinguishing the Signal from
the Noise*

WHEN IT COMES TO INVESTING, WE SEEM TO BE ADDICTED
TO INFORMATION. The whole investment industry is obsessed
with learning more and more about less and less, until we
know absolutely everything about nothing. Rarely, if ever,
do we stop to consider how much information we actually need to know in order to make a decision. As Daniel
J. Boorstin opined, "The greatest obstacle to discovery is
not ignorance—it is the illusion of knowledge."

The idea that more information must be better seems obvious. After all, if the information is of no use, then it can simply be ignored. However, psychological studies cast doubt on the soundness of this seemingly innocuous belief.

Is More Better?

In one study,* eight experienced bookmakers were shown a list of 88 variables found on a typical past performance chart of a racehorse (e.g., the weight to be carried, the number of races won, the performance in different conditions, and so on). Each bookmaker was then asked to rank the pieces of information by importance.

Having done this, the bookmakers were then given data for 45 past races and asked to rank the top five horses in each race.

Each bookmaker was given the past data in increments of the 5, 10, 20, and 40 variables he had selected as most important. Hence each bookmaker predicted the outcome of each race four times—once for each of the information sets. For each prediction the bookmakers were asked to give a degree of confidence ranking in their forecast.

With five pieces of information, accuracy and confidence were quite closely related. Sadly, as more and more

*P. Slovic, "Behavioral Problems Adhering to a Decision Policy" (Unpublished paper, 1973).

information was made available, two things happened. First, accuracy flat-lined. The bookmakers were as accurate when they had five pieces of information as when they had 40 items to help them. So much for more information helping people make better decisions.

Secondly, the degree of confidence expressed in the forecast increased massively with information. With five pieces of information the bookmakers were around 17 percent confident; by the time they had 40 items of information, confidence had exploded up to more than 30 percent (without any improvement in accuracy, remember!). So all the extra information wasn't making the bookmakers any more accurate, but it was making them increasingly overconfident.

Another group of psychologists have recently found very similar patterns when it comes to American football.* They tested football fans' ability to predict the outcome and point spread in 15 NCAA games. In order to take part in the study, participants had to pass a test demonstrating that they were highly knowledgeable about college football. Thus, the subjects could safely be described as experts.

The information (selected by surveying non-participating football fans) was presented in a random order over five

*C. Tsai, J. Kalyman, and R. Hastie, "Effects of Amount of Information on Judgment Accuracy and Confidence" (Working paper, 2007).

rounds. Each round revealed six items of information in a random order. The information provided deliberately excluded team names, since these were too leading. Instead, the items covered a wide range of statistics on football such as fumbles, turnover margin, and yards gained.

To see if more information really was better information, a computer model was given the same data as the humans. In each round, the computer model was given more information, replicating the conditions the human players faced.

The results are reassuring for those who argue that more is always preferable to less. With just the first set of information (six items) the computer model was about 56 percent accurate. As more information was gradually added, the predictive accuracy rose to 71 percent. So for the computer, more information truly was better.

What about the humans? Much like the bookmakers, the football experts' accuracy didn't improve with additional information. It didn't matter whether they had 6 or 30 items of information; their accuracy was about the same. However, the participants' confidence soared as more information was added. For instance, participants started off at 69 percent confident with 6 pieces of information, and rose to nearly 80 percent confident by the time they had 30 items of information. Just as with the bookmakers, confidence but not accuracy increased with the amount of information available.

When Less Is More

Why was there such a difference between the computer and the humans? We humans have limits on our ability to process information. We simply aren't supercomputers that can carry out massive amounts of calculations in a fraction of a second. We have limited processing capacity.

More evidence of these bounds was provided by a recent study on choosing cars.* In the study, participants were asked to choose between four different cars. They faced one of two conditions; they were either given just 4 attributes per car or 12 attributes per car. In both cases, one of the cars was noticeably better than the others, with some 75 percent of its attributes being positive. Two cars had 50 percent positive attributes and one car had only 25 percent. With only a low level of information, nearly 60 percent of subjects chose the best car. However, when faced with information overload (12 attributes to try and think about and juggle), only around 20 percent of subjects chose the best car.

*A. Dijksterhuis, M. Bos, L. Nordgren, and R. Van Baaren, "On Making the Right Choice: The Deliberation Without Attention Effect," *Science* 311 (2007): 1005–1007.

A similar outcome was found among financial analysts.* The task they were given was to forecast fourth-quarter earnings in 45 cases. In fact, there were 15 firms, but each firm was presented in one of three different information formats. The information formats were:

1. Baseline data consisting of the past three quarters of EPS, net sales, and stock price.
2. Baseline data plus redundant or irrelevant information, that is, information that was already embodied in the baseline data such as the PE ratio.
3. Baseline data plus nonredundant information that should have improved forecasting ability, such as the fact that the dividend was increased.

None of the participants realized that they had all seen the same company in three different formats, perhaps because each presentation was separated by at least seven other profiles.

Each respondent was not only asked for his or her forecast but also for their confidence in their forecast. Both redundant and nonredundant information significantly increased the forecast error. However, guess what? The

*F.D. Davis, G.L. Lohse, and J.E. Kotteman, "Harmful Effects of Seemingly Helpful Information on Forecasts of Stock Earnings," *Journal of Economic Psychology* 15 (1994): 253–267.

self-reported confidence ratings for each of the forecasts increased massively with the amount of information that was available.

From the Emergency Room to the Markets

Given my earlier comments on the problems of confidence in the medical profession, you might be inclined to say that there is little that investors could possibly learn from doctors. However, you would be wrong, and here is why.

Our tale starts in a hospital in Michigan. Physicians at this particular hospital tended to send about 90 percent of all patients with severe chest pains to the cardiac care unit. The unit was becoming seriously overcrowded, care standards were dropping, and costs were rising.

The decision to send so many patients to the ICU reflected concerns among doctors over the costs of a false negative (i.e., not admitting someone who should have been admitted). Fine, you might say, rather an overcrowded hospital than the alternative. But this ignores the risks inherent in entering the ICU. About 20 thousand Americans die every year from a hospital-transmitted illness. The risks of contracting such a disease are markedly higher in an ICU than in a conventional ward.

The most damning problem for the Michigan hospital doctors was that they sent about 90 percent of those who needed to be admitted and also 90 percent of those who didn't need to be admitted to an ICU. They did no better than chance!

Such a performance begs the question of why doctors found it so difficult to separate those who needed specialist care from those that didn't. Luckily, this question has been examined.*

The researchers studying this problem uncovered a startling fact—the doctors were looking at the wrong factors. They tended to overweigh risk factors such as a family history of premature coronary artery disease, age, male gender, smoking, diabetes mellitus, increased serum cholesterol, and hypertension.

While looking at these risk factors helps assess the overall likelihood of someone having cardiac ischemia, they have little diagnostic power. They are what might be called pseudo-diagnostic items. Far better diagnostic cues are available. Research has revealed that the nature and location of patients' symptoms, their history of ischemic disease, and certain specific electrocardiographic findings are by far the most powerful predictors of acute ischemia, infarction, and mortality. It is these factors that the doctors should be looking at, rather than the risk factors that they were actually paying attention to.

*L. Green and J. Yates, "Influence of Pseudodiagnostic Information on the Evaluation of Ischemic Heart Disease," *Annals of Emergency Medicine* 25 (1995): 451–457.

Could anything be done to help doctors look at the right things? The researchers came up with the idea of using laminated cards with various probabilities marked against diagnostic information. The doctors could then follow these tables and multiply the probabilities according to the symptoms and test findings in order to estimate the overall likelihood of a problem. If this was above a set threshold, then the patient was to be admitted to cardiac ICU; otherwise a normal bed with a monitor would suffice.

After this aid to decision was introduced there was a marked improvement in the decision-making of the doctors. They still caught a high proportion of problem cases, but they cut down dramatically on sending patients to ICU who didn't need to go.

Of course, this might indicate the aid had worked. But, being good and conscientious scientists, Green and colleagues decided they had better check to ensure that this was the case. This was done by giving the doctors the decision tool in some weeks and not giving it to them in other weeks. Obviously, if the tool was the source of the improved performance, one would expect some deterioration in performance in the weeks when access to the aid was prohibited.

The results from this experiment showed something surprising. Decision-making seemed to have improved regardless of the use of the tool. What could account for this surprising finding? Was it possible that doctors had memorized the probabilities from the cards, and were using them even when the cards weren't available? This seemed unlikely, since the various combinations and permutations listed on the card were not easy to recall. In fact, the doctors had managed to assimilate the correct cues. That is to say, by showing them the correct items to use for diagnosis, the doctors' emphasis switched from pseudo-diagnostic information to truly informative elements. They started looking at the right things!

Based on this experience, the researchers designed a very easy-to-use decision aid—a series of yes/no questions. If the patient displayed a particular electrocardiogram anomaly (the ST change), they were admitted to ICU straight away. If not, a second cue was considered: whether the patient was suffering chest pains. If they were, they were again admitted to ICU, and so forth. This aid made the critical elements of the decision transparent and salient to the doctor.

These simple checklists also worked exceptionally well in practice. The simple yes/no questions actually improved both the number of patients correctly sent to ICU (95 percent) and reduced the number incorrectly sent to ICU down to 50 percent. That was even better than the complex statistical model.

The power of simple checklists should not be underestimated. One very recent study* examined how the implementation of a simple 19-point surgical checklist might help save lives. The checklist covered things as simple as making sure someone had checked that this was the same patient everyone thought it was, that the nurses had reconfirmed the sterility of all the instruments, and that at the end of surgery, someone counted all the instruments and made sure the number was the same as at the start of the operation.

These might sound like the kinds of things you hope would occur anyway. However, having the checklist forced people to go through the steps. The results of this checklist implementation were astounding. Prior to the introduction of the checklist the patient death rate was 1.8 percent and the complication post surgery rate was 11 percent. After the checklist was introduced the death rate dropped to 0.8 percent and the complication rate collapsed to 7 percent.

But, enough about doctors and their patients—what can investors learn from all of this? Simple: It is far better to focus on what really matters, rather than succumbing to the siren call of Wall Street's many noise peddlers.

*A.B. Haynes et al., "A Surgical Safety Checklist to Reduce Morbidity and Mortality in a Global Population," *New England Journal of Medicine* 360 (2009): 491–499.

We would be far better off analyzing the five things we really need to know about an investment, rather than trying to know absolutely everything about everything concerned with the investment.

Jean-Marie Eveillard of First Eagle affirms my contention by saying, "It's very common to drown in the details or be attracted to complexity, but what's most important to me is to know what three, four, or five major characteristics of the business really matter. I see my job primarily as asking the right questions and focusing the analysis in order to make a decision."

Another great investor who knows how to distinguish the signal from the noise is, of course, Warren Buffett. You'll never hear him discuss the earnings outlook over the next quarter or consult an overabundance of information when making an investment. Instead he says "Our method is very simple. We just try to buy businesses with good-to-superb underlying economics run by honest and able people and buy them at sensible prices. That's all I'm trying to do."

There is no one right approach to investing, nor are there three, four, or five factors I can tell you to always evaluate when making an investment. It all depends on your investment approach. I'm a deep value investor, so my favorite focus points might not be to your tastes. I essentially focus upon three elements:

1. Valuation: Is this stock seriously undervalued?
2. Balance sheets: Is this stock going bust?
3. Capital discipline: What is the management doing with the cash I'm giving them?

These points may or may not be useful to you in your approach to investing, but the important take-away here is that you should determine the factors you will use to assess your investment choices, and then you will focus on your own analysis of each of these elements.

Chapter Seven

Turn off That Bubblevision!

~

Volatility Equals Opportunity

ON ANY GIVEN DAY I CAN TURN ON THE TV and find at least three channels dedicated to filling my mind with in-depth analysis of what are near random fluctuations in the markets. As I mentioned earlier, these channels are described by a friend as bubblevision. The minutiae of the daily moves are explained to the rest of us by a combination of attractive women and impassioned men, with a smattering of bow-tie-wearing experts to aid credibility.

The same thing happens in the financial press; column after column is filled with ex-post justifications for why the market did whatever it did yesterday.

As we discussed in the last chapter, too much information leads us to feel overconfident in the extreme, but it does little to aid us. But this isn't our only problem with information; we actually find even useless information soothing and we process it mindlessly.

For example, psychologists have explored the role of "placebic" information in people's behavior.* Placebic information is simply words that mean nothing. Could such redundant information really impact anyone's behavior?

The psychologists set up a clever experiment by waiting for a queue to form at a photocopier and having a confederate try to butt into the line. Three possible excuses for jumping the line were provided:

1. "Excuse me, I have five pages. May I use the Xerox machines?" The no-information case.
2. "Excuse me, I have five pages. May I use the Xerox machine, because I have to make copies?" The placebic case—after all, everyone in the line

*E.J. Langer, A. Blank, and B. Chanowitz, "The Mindlessness of Ostensibly Thoughtful Action: The Role of Placebic Information in Interpersonal Interaction," *Journal of Personality and Social Psychology* 36 (1978): 635–642.

needs to make copies or they wouldn't be in the
line.

3. "Excuse me, I have five pages. May I use the Xerox
machine, because I'm in a rush?" Real information.

A surprisingly high 60 percent of people allowed the
confederate to jump the line even without any information
given. When placebic or real information was given, the
compliance rate rose to over 90 percent. By simply using
the word "because" in a sentence, someone was able to
persuade people to believe that the justification was true
and meaningful. We appear to like reasons, however banal
they may be.

The same psychologists went on to conduct a second
experiment in which they rummaged around the secretaries' rubbish bins at the Graduate Center of the City
University of New York. They collected a sample of
memos to give them an idea of the kind of information
that the secretaries would receive on a daily basis. Having
determined this, the experimenters then sent mock memos
from a nonexistent person. The memos simply asked for
the memo itself to be returned to a certain room at the
university—a totally futile exercise, but I'm sure it's familiar to those who work in large organizations.

It was hypothesized that when the information arrived
in a fashion that the secretaries would regard as normal

they would respond in a mindless fashion. Having looked at the style of memos the secretaries regularly received, the experimenters thought that impersonal requests would be the most common form of memo encountered.

The results bore out the researchers' viewpoint. When the secretaries received an impersonal request style memo, 90 percent of them followed the instruction to return the memo to another room in the university via the internal mail.

A few years ago I came across another great example of people's malleability. The Catholic Church had conducted a poll of 1000 people, which revealed that those who had read the *Da Vinci Code* were twice as likely to believe that Jesus Christ fathered children, and four times as likely to believe that Opus Dei was a murderous sect, than those who hadn't read the book.

All this evidence strongly suggests that when people see information in a format with which they are familiar, they will unquestioningly process it. Hence, the survival of what can only be described as noise peddlers in financial markets. Investors faced with chronic uncertainty will turn to any vaguely plausible explanation and cling to it.

Meet Mr. Market

As we saw in Chapter 5, the power of the outside view can be harnessed to help mitigate our otherwise mindless processing. When it comes to the vagaries of the ups and downs of financial markets, Larry Summers provides us with the outside view. He co-authored a paper* in 1989 that explored the 50 largest moves in the U.S. stock market between 1947 and 1987. Summers and colleagues scoured the press to see if they could find any reason for the market moves.

They concluded "On most of the sizable return days . . . the information that the press cites as the cause of the market move is not particularly important. Press reports on adjacent days also fail to reveal any convincing accounts of why future profits or discount rates might have changed." To put it another way, more than half of the largest moves in markets are totally unrelated to anything that might be classed as fundamentals.

Price volatility is a fact of life in financial markets. Ben Graham described the reality of excessive volatility as being in business with a partner named Mr. Market—a very obliging chap.

> Every day he tells you what he thinks your interest is worth and furthermore offers either to buy you out or to sell you an additional interest . . . Sometimes

*D.M. Cutler, J. Poterba, and L.H. Summers, "What Moves Stock Prices?" *Journal of Portfolio Management* 15 (Spring 1989): 4–13.

his ideas of value appears plausible and justified by business developments and prospects as you know them. Often, on the other hand, Mr. Market lets his enthusiasm or his fears run away with him, and the value he proposes seems to you little short of silly.

In short, Mr. Market is a chronic manic depressive (or suffers from bipolar disorder, as it is now known). Those who focus upon market price for investment advice are doomed to failure. John Maynard Keynes pointed out the irony of the situation: "It is largely the fluctuations which throw up bargains and the uncertainty due to the fluctuations which prevents other people from taking advantage of them."

Of course, this volatility is the very reason why bubblevision exists. If markets were dull and boring there would be nothing for the commentators to talk about.

What can we do to protect ourselves against these noise peddlers? One of my former clients had a novel solution. They have just one Bloomberg terminal in their entire office. Anyone approaching the dreaded machine is subject to ritual humiliation. They view the noise as massively counterproductive to their efforts as investors. Turning off the bubblevision is a great step towards preventing yourself from becoming a slave to the market.

Chapter Eight

See No Evil, Hear No Evil

~

It's Time to Prove Yourself Wrong

Tɪᴍᴇ ꜰᴏʀ ᴀɴᴏᴛʜᴇʀ ʙʀᴀɪɴ ᴛᴇᴀsᴇʀ.

Let's imagine that you have four playing cards laid out in front of you. Each one has a letter on one side and a number on the other. The four face-up symbols are E, 4, K, and 7. I'm going to tell you that if a card has an E then it should have a 4 on the reverse. Which cards would you like to turn over to see if I am telling the truth?

Give it a little thought.

If you are like an incredible 95 percent of the fund managers who have answered this question, you will get it wrong. So no pressure then!

This question has by far and away the highest failure rate out of any question that I ask. It is also one of those biases that are immune to your performance on the cognitive reflection task we covered in Chapter 1. No matter how well you scored, the chances are you will still suffer the bias that underlies this problem.

The most common answer is E and 4. The correct answer is that you do need to turn two cards over, and they are the E and the 7. Let me explain. Most people get the E; if you turn it over and it doesn't have a 4 on the back you have proven that I lied. If you turn the 7 over and it has an E on the back, you would have also proven that I lied. However, turning the 4 over can't help you. I said that E had to have a 4, not that 4 had to have an E. The habit of going for the 4 is known as confirmatory bias—looking for the evidence that agrees with us.

Let's try another one. Imagine you are faced with the following sequence of numbers: 2-4-6. Your job is to figure out the rule I used to construct this sequence. To uncover the rule you may construct other sets of three numbers and I will give you feedback as to whether they satisfy the rule I used. If you are sure you have the solution, you may stop testing and tell me what you think the rule is.

Most people approach this test by suggesting 4-6-8, to which the response is "Yes, it fits the rule," then 10-12-14, which again garners a positive response. Many people think they know the rule at this point, and say something along the lines of "Any numbers that increase in increments of two," or "Even numbers that increase by increments of two," to all of which the response is, "That isn't the rule I used to construct the sequences."

In fact, the rule used was "Any ascending numbers," but very, very few people ever manage to uncover the rule. The easiest way of doing so is to identify sequences that generate the response, "No, that doesn't fit the rule," such as a sequence of descending numbers or a mixed order of numbers. But most of us simply don't think to suggest these kinds of sequences. Again, we are too busy looking for information that confirms our hypothesis.

This behavioral pitfall of looking for confirming rather than disconfirming evidence is in direct violation of the principles outlined by Karl Popper, the philosopher of science. He argued that the only way to test a hypothesis was to look for all the information that disagreed with it—a process known as falsification.

Charles Darwin often looked for disconfirming evidence. Every time he came across a fact that seemed to contradict his theory of evolution he wrote it down and tried to figure out how it fit in. Unfortunately, not many investors are like Darwin.

Confirmatory bias is all too common a mistake when it comes to investing and other spheres as well. In fact, it transpires that we are twice as likely to look for information that agrees with us than we are to seek out disconfirming evidence. Who do we choose to read? The people who agree with us most. Dick Cheney reportedly insists that the hotel TV is set to Fox news before he will enter it! Who do we like to have meetings with? The people with the ideas closest to our own. Why? Because it makes us feel warm and fuzzy as human beings to have our own ideas repeated back to us and at the end of the meeting we can all leave agreeing that we are all very smart.

This is a lousy way of testing a view. Instead, we should sit down with the people who disagree with us most. Not so that we will change our minds, because the odds of changing one's mind through a simple conversation are about a million to one against, but rather so that we can hear the opposite side of the argument. If we can't find the logical flaw in the argument, we have no business holding our view as strongly as we probably do.

The Sorry Tale of Sir Roger

Not only do we look for information that agrees with us, but we tend to see all information as supporting our hypothesis. An extreme example of this tendency is provided in the pitiful but true tale of Sir Roger Tichborne. In 1854, Sir Roger was reported as lost at sea. His mother refused to believe that her son, whom she had lovingly raised in France, was gone forever. She kept putting out inquiries, asking for any news of her son.

Twelve years after the loss of Sir Roger, it appeared that Lady Tichborne's prayers had been answered. She received a letter from an Australian lawyer claiming to have found her son. The letter explained that, having been shipwrecked, Sir Roger eventually made his way to Australia, where he became involved in a series of business ventures after having vowed to make a success of himself following his miraculous escape. Unfortunately, the businesses did not work as well as he expected, and he had been too embarrassed to contact his mother.

However, he had recently seen her inquiries and was filled with remorse for the worry he had caused her over the years. The letter concluded with a request to send money for the travel fare of Sir Roger, his wife, and children. Lady Tichborne was delighted to hear this news, and sent the relevant monies to allow for the family reunion.

When Sir Roger arrived in England he was received by Lady Tichborne as her long lost son, and granted a stipend of £1,000 annually.

However, not all the Tichborne family were convinced that this new arrival was the real Sir Roger. After all, they reasoned, Sir Roger had been a lithe man of slim frame, but the new arrival was obese in the extreme (to see pictures go to www3.hants.gov.uk/museum/community-history/tichborne-claimant.htm). While people can change their size, it is rare that tattoos disappear—Sir Roger had some, the new arrival had none. Nor is it easy to change one's eye color—Sir Roger had blue eyes, the new arrival had brown eyes. He was also an inch taller than Sir Roger had been, didn't speak French (which Sir Roger did), and had a birthmark on his torso, which Sir Roger didn't.

Somehow Lady Tichborne managed to ignore all this evidence. It was only after her death that the family finally managed to show that the Australian import was an impostor. He ended up serving ten years for imposture and perjury.

Prisoners of Our Preconceptions

While the tale of Lady Tichborne's blindness to evidence is extreme, we often find lesser examples. For instance, a group of people were asked to read randomly selected studies on the deterrent efficacy of the death sentence (and criticisms of those studies).* Subjects were also asked to rate the studies in terms of the impact they had on their views on capital punishment and deterrence. Half of the people were pro-death penalty and half were anti-death penalty.

Those who started with a pro-death sentence stance thought the studies that supported capital punishment were well argued, sound, and important. They also thought the studies that argued against the death penalty were all deeply flawed. Those who held the opposite point of view at the outset reached exactly the opposite conclusion. As the psychologists concluded, "Asked for their final attitudes relative to the experiment's start, proponents reported they were more in favor of capital punishment, whereas opponents reported that they were less in favor of capital punishment." In effect each participant's views polarized, becoming much more extreme than before the experiment.

In another study of biased assimilation† (accepting all evidence as supporting your case), participants were told a soldier at Abu Ghraib prison was charged with

*M.R. Leeper, C.G. Lord, and L. Ross, "Biased Assimilation and Attitude Polarization: The Effects of Prior Theories on Subsequently Considered Evidence," *Journal of Personality and Social Psychology* 37 (1979): 2098–2109.
†D. Westen, P. Blagov, J. Feit, P. Arkowitz, and P. Thagard, "When Reason and Passion Collide: Emotional Constraint Satisfaction in Motivated Political Reasoning" (Unpublished working paper, 2004).

torturing prisoners. He wanted the right to subpoena senior administration officials. He claimed he'd been informed that the administration had suspended the Geneva Convention.

The psychologists gave different people different amounts of evidence supporting the soldier's claims. For some, the evidence was minimal; for others, it was overwhelming. Unfortunately, the amount of evidence was essentially irrelevant in assessing people's behavior. For 84 percent of the time, it was possible to predict whether people believed the evidence was sufficient to subpoena Donald Rumsfeld based on just three things:

1. The extent to which they liked Republicans.
2. The extent to which they liked the U.S. military.
3. The extent to which they liked human rights groups like Amnesty International.

Adding the evidence into the equation allowed the researchers to increase the prediction accuracy from 84 to 85 percent.

Time and again, psychologists have found that confidence and biased assimilation perform a strange tango. It appears the more sure people were that they had the correct view, the more they distorted new evidence to suit their existing preference, which in turn made them even more confident.

Kill the Company

So, what can we do to defend our finances against this insidious tendency to look for the information that agrees with us? The obvious answer is that we need to learn to look for evidence that would prove our own analysis wrong. Robert Williamson, one of the many successful offspring from Julian Robertson's Tiger and co-manager of Williamson McAree Investment Partners, affirms, "Julian Robertson was always adamant about seeking out the opposite point of view and then being completely honest with yourself in deciding whether your analysis overrides that. That's something we try to practice every day."

But like most behavioral biases, while the answer may be relatively obvious, actually practicing the solution is generally much harder.

One investor really stands out as having tried to protect himself against the dangers of confirmatory bias: Bruce Berkowitz of Fairholme Capital Management. Rather than looking for all the information that would support an investment, Berkowitz tries to kill the company. He says:

> We look at companies, count the cash, and try to kill the company. . . . We spend a lot of time thinking about what could go wrong with a company—whether it's a recession, stagflation, zooming interest rates or a dirty bomb going off. We try every which way

to kill our best ideas. If we can't kill it, maybe we're onto something. If you go with companies that are prepared for difficult times, especially if they are linked to managers who are engineered for difficult times, then you almost want those times because they plant the seeds of greatness.

Berkowitz goes further and even provides a list of ways in which: "Companies die and how they're killed . . . Here are the ways you implode: you don't generate cash, you burn cash, you're over-leveraged, you play Russian Roulette, you have idiots for management, you have a bad board, you 'de-worsify,' you buy your stock too high, you lie with GAAP accounting."

I suspect that investors could learn much from the approach that Berkowitz espouses. It essentially turns the investment viewpoint upside down (much like the reverse engineered DCF that we saw in Chapter 5). By looking at the ways in which things can go wrong, rather than looking for all the evidence that everything is going well, Berkowitz is protecting himself, and like all pessimists stands to be surprised by the upside—never a bad thing—rather than surprised by the downside.

Chapter Nine

In the Land of the Perma-Bear and the Perma-Bull

When the Facts Change, Change Your Mind

Time for another game for you to puzzle over.

Imagine two urns filled with millions of poker chips. In one of the urns, 70 percent of the chips are red and 30 percent are blue. In the other, the ratio is reversed, so we have 70 percent blue and 30 percent red chips. Suppose one of the urns is chosen randomly and a dozen chips are drawn from it: eight red chips and four blue chips. What are the chances that the chips came from the urn with mostly red chips? (Give your answer as a percentage.)

If you are like most people, you have probably just said a figure between 70 and 80 percent. Surprisingly, the correct answer is actually a whopping 97 percent. To arrive at this answer you would need to apply Bayes Theorem, a relatively simple formula which shows how the probability that a theory is true is affected by a new piece of evidence. However, very few people solve this problem correctly. They end up being too conservative.

This tendency towards conservatism isn't just seen in odd mathematical problems. It rears its head in the real world as well. Doug Kass of Seabreeze wrote an article for *RealMoney Silver* on May 27, 2009, which summed up the problem of conservatism very well. In this piece, Kass warns of the dangers of being a perma-bull—always bullish on the market—or a perma-bear—always negative on the market.

I have often written that both perma-bears and perma-bulls are attention-getters, not money-makers. The perma-bear cult, of which I have often been accused of being a member, never ever or rarely make money. Ironically, the perma-bear crowd is typically uninhabited by money managers. For example, the largest and highest profile short seller, Kynikos' Jim Chanos, is not a perma-bear. Jim systematically searches for broken or breaking business models, and he understands market and company-specific risk/reward.

Rather than managing money, the perma-bear crowd is typically inhabited by writers of market letters, investment strategists and economists turned strategists, all of whom have little or no skin in the game. They also make a lot of speeches during downturns for a helluva lot of money and often write editorials in the *Financial Times*, *New York Times* and *Wall Street Journal*.

By contrast, the job of a money manager is not to be dogmatic . . . neither is it to make friends; it is to make money. The perma-bear species is a fickle breed, especially in its ardor for purging from its ranks anyone who breaks the faith. Woe betide a former perma-bear deemed less bearish!

In summary, perma-bears, similar to their first cousin perma-bulls, rarely make money and, in the main, shouldn't be listened to most of the time as even when they call a downturn, they almost always overstay their positions. And they may be harmful to your financial health.

I can certainly sympathize with Kass' viewpoints on the dangers posed to "perma-bears" who turn bullish. Having been cautious on the markets for a number of years, as detailed in Chapter 2, I turned bullish in late 2008, and thought that markets (especially outside the United States) were generally very cheap in March 2009. When I expressed this viewpoint, I found that I actually got hate mail from "perma-bear" clients.

I also have firsthand experience of conservatism at work. In the past I was part of an asset allocation team at an investment bank. Every so often we would get together to discuss our views. This usually involved a trip to the local pub (possibly not the best place for such discussions), where we'd have a couple of pints to put us in the mood for talking. Then we'd proceed to discuss where we had been right (which didn't take very long), where we had been wrong (which took much longer), and finally we would end up discussing why we'd been wrong, and how we would be right in the near future! Let me assure you that this was a very pleasant way of spending an afternoon—but a lousy way of making decisions.

We were displaying classic conservatism—hanging on to our views too long and only adjusting them slowly.

We were far from alone in suffering from conservatism. In one study of psychologists by a psychologist* (surely a definition of twisted), the participants were given a profile of a young man, Joseph Kidd, who was seeking clinical psychological help.

In the first stage, the psychologists were given just a very brief demographic-based analysis of Kidd. They were told he was 29 years old, white, unmarried, and a veteran of World War II. They were also informed that he was a college graduate who now works as a business assistant in a floral decorating studio.

At the end of each presentation, the psychologists had to answer questions on Kidd's behavioral patterns, attitudes, interests, and typical reactions to real-life events. Stage I was deliberately minimal to establish a base rate with which to compare later stages. Stage II added one and a half pages of information about Kidd's childhood through the age of 12. Stage III was two pages on his high school and college experiences. The final stage of information covered his army service and later life up to the present day.

If you read the previous chapters carefully, I'm pretty sure you should have an idea of the kinds of patterns that were found. Average accuracy after the first stage was

*S. Oskamp, "Overconfidence in Case-Study Judgements," *Journal of Consulting Psychology* 29 (1965): 261–265.

just over 25 percent, but by the end of Stage III average final accuracy was less than 28 percent. Despite the fact that accuracy increases only marginally as the information increases, confidence explodes (as we saw in other studies in Chapter 7). It soared from an average of 33 percent in Stage I to an average of 53 percent in Stage IV.

More interesting is that the number of psychologists who changed their minds at each stage was also monitored. As the amount of information increased, so the number of participants changing their minds dropped from 40 percent in Stage II to just 25 percent in Stage IV. As the researcher concluded, the psychologists may frequently have formed stereotype conclusions rather firmly from their first fragmentary information and then been reluctant to change their conclusions as they received new information. Or put another way, the psychologists made up their minds early on, and then refused to change them. This is a great example of the interaction between conservatism and confirmatory bias from the last chapter.

Hanging onto Your View

This behavioral pitfall—hanging onto your view too long—is observed frequently in the financial world. For instance, Exhibit 9.1 shows that analysts are exceptionally good at one thing, and possibly one thing alone—telling you what has just happened.

EXHIBIT 9.1   Analysts Lag Reality

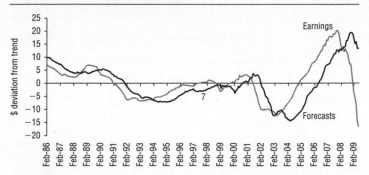

Source: GMO.

Exhibit 9.1 was constructed by detrending operating earnings and the analyst forecasts of those earnings so that the chart plots deviations from trend in dollars-per-share terms. It clearly shows that analysts lag reality. They only change their mind when there is irrefutable proof they were wrong, and then they only change their minds very slowly—a process known as anchoring and slow adjustment.

In many ways, 2008 was a case study in financial conservatism. The recession that was engulfing all the major economies was eerily like watching a slow motion train wreck. The head of research at the investment bank I was working at used some of my work to show the analysts that they were always behind the curve and incite them to do better. The analysts seemed to be able to grasp this, and went away to cut their numbers. Of course, the first thing they did was talk to their companies (as if they knew anything more than the rest of us—but that is another story). The companies unsurprisingly said the recession wouldn't affect them (even the cyclically exposed ones). After hearing this, the analysts came back to us and said, "We can't cut our numbers!"

The following excerpts from companies' press releases typified the attitude. The first comes from a company that describes themselves as a specialist in "industry specific solutions (Banking, Human Resources and Real Estate)":

We have made the right choices in positioning and we have implemented a successful business model fuelled not only by technological development but also by both the trend towards outsourcing and enterprise consolidation. We don't believe that our business model is subject to a cyclical downturn that is often talked about these days.

However, I think my personal favorite is this one:

We are mindful of current investor concerns about the economy. However, our forecast continues to support our confidence in our ability to execute our plan . . . These customer initiatives have been driving investment in our solutions for at least two years, and we believe customers would only accelerate them in a more difficult economic environment.

Essentially this company is saying that a recession is just what their business needs (and they weren't receivers!). This kind of statement reminds me of a twisted science experiment in which you dose rats with radiation, and then conclude that the ones that survive are stronger. Well, they are stronger than the ones that didn't survive, but they sure aren't stronger than before they were dosed with radiation!

These kinds of statements help explain why we rarely see analysts go from buy to sell or vice versa. Generally, a smoother transition of recommendations is observed: buy to add to hold to reduce to sell. Of course, by the time the stock reaches sell it is usually time to buy it again.

The classic study on conservatism* (from which the urn example at the start of this chapter was drawn) concludes its analysis by saying: "A convenient first approximation to the data would say that it takes anywhere from two to five observations to do one observation's worth in inducing the subject to change their opinions." In other words,

---

*Ward Edwards, "Conservatism in Human Information Processing," (1968), reprinted in Kahneman, Slovic, and Tversky, *Judgement under Uncertainty: Heuristics and Biases* (Cambridge University Press, 1982).

people underreact to things that should make them change their minds. That certainly seems to sum up the average analyst.

I should also point out that it appears that people are particularly bad at spotting regime changes. Researchers* have shown that in a series of experiments using urns like in the question above, people tend to underreact in unstable environments with precise signals (turning points), but overreact to stable environments with noisy signals (trending markets). This helps explain why economists and analysts tend to miss turning points in the market. They get hung up on the stable environment and overreact to it; hence they miss the important things that happen when the environment becomes more unstable (a recession starts) and underreact to such developments.

Sunk Costs at the Root of Conservatism

So why are analysts and the rest of us so reticent to alter views? What is the root cause of this conservatism? The answer seems to me to lie in the "sunk cost" fallacy. This is a tendency to allow past unrecoverable expenses to inform current decisions. Brutally put, we tend to hang onto our views too long simply because we spent time and effort in coming up with those views in the first place.

*C. Massy and G. Wu, "Detecting Regime Shifts: The Causes of Under- and Overreaction," *Management Science* 51 (2005): 932–947.

For instance, consider the following scenario:* As the president of an airline company, you have invested 10 million dollars of the company's money into a research project. The purpose was to build a plane that would not be detected by conventional radar—in other words, a stealth plane. When the project is 90 percent completed, another firm begins marketing a plane that cannot be detected by radar. Also, it is apparent that their plane is much faster and far more economical than the plane your company is building. The question is: Should you invest the last 10 percent of the research funds to finish your stealth plane?

Well over 80 percent of respondents reply they would invest the last 10 percent of the research funds to finish the stealth plane.

Now consider this scenario: As the president of an airline company, you have received a suggestion from one of your employees. The suggestion is to use the last $1 million of your research funds to develop a plane that would not be detected by conventional radar, in other words, a stealth plane. However, another firm has just begun marketing a plane that cannot be detected by radar. Also, it is apparent that their plane is much faster and far more

*H. Arkes and C. Blumer, "The Psychology of Sunk Costs," *Organizational Behavior and Human Decision Processes* 35 (1985): 124–140.

economical than the plane your company could build. The question is: Should you invest the last million dollars of your research funds to build the radar-blank plane proposed by your employee?

This time around more than 80 percent of respondents said no.

There is very little material difference between these two questions. However, the first activates a sunk cost frame—we have already committed funds to the project; whereas the second scenario features no such prior commitment. This simple change has a truly massive impact upon the answers given. This highlights the power of the sunk cost and its role in creating conservatism.

What can we do to guard against conservatism?

Earlier I talked about the way in which one of my former team had analyzed our asset allocation decisions. Rather than hanging onto our views, what we should have done is give ourselves a blank sheet of paper, imagine our positions were zero, and say to ourselves "Given what we now know, would we open a fresh long or new short?" If the answer is yes and it corresponds to a position, then fine. However, if the answer is no, but the position is still running, then it should be closed out.

We should all be encouraged to revisit our investment cases and approach them with a blank slate. Are they built on bad assumptions (i.e., continued margin expansion)?

Do we still believe them to be true? Or did we miss something? If it is the latter, perhaps an analyst amnesty, with no recriminations for changing recommendations, might help remove the conservatism bias.

Of course, giving yourself a blank sheet of paper is easy to say but difficult to do. So an alternative method might be a spot of job switching. In a professional setting, analysts should look over their colleagues' investment cases, rather than their own, and offer any adverse insight. This should help alleviate the anchoring on a position simply because it is your own position.

Another approach to defeating conservatism is to play a game of devil's advocate, where certain people purposely construct the opposing point of view and question their ideas against yours. Edward Studzinski of Oakmark is a fan of this approach to ameliorating the problem of conservatism.

We have periodic devil's-advocate reviews of all our large holdings and a separate analyst is charged with presenting the negative case. It's more than a debate society, the devil's advocate should genuinely believe the negative argument is the right one. We obviously make plenty of mistakes, but that discipline helps us reduce the frequency and severity of them. In investing, that's half the battle.

Michael Steinhardt, the legendary hedge fund manager, had perhaps the most extreme response conservatism. In his autobiography, *No Bull*, Steinhardt writes:

> I tried to view the portfolio fresh every day . . . Irregularly . . . I would decide I did not like the portfolio writ large. I did not think we were in sync with the market, and while there were various degrees of conviction on individual securities, I concluded we would be better off with a clean slate. I would call either . . . Goldman Sachs . . . or Salomon Brothers and ask to have us taken out of the entire portfolio. In swift trade, one of these firms would buy our longs and cover our shorts . . . In an instant, I would have a clean position sheet. Sometimes it felt refreshing to start over, all in cash, and to build a portfolio of names that represented our strongest convictions and cut us free from wishy-washy holdings.

While the idea of selling the entire portfolio may sound a little extreme, it shows the discipline that is needed to overcome our behavioral biases. Hanging onto a view simply because it is your view is likely to end in tears. As Keynes said "When the facts change I change my mind, what do you do sir?"

Chapter Ten

The Siren Song of Stories

Focusing on the Facts

Of all the dangers that investors face, perhaps none is more seductive than the siren song of stories. Stories essentially govern the way we think. We will abandon evidence in favour of a good story. Taleb calls this tendency to be suckered by stories the narrative fallacy. As he writes in *The Black Swan*, "The fallacy is associated with our vulnerability to over-interpretation and our predilection for compact stories over raw truths. It severely distorts our mental representation of the world."

To illustrate the danger of stories, let's imagine you are a juror serving on a first degree murder trial. This is a trial like any other trial; the prosecution and the defense both present their cases. However, rather than deliberating as a jury you just write down whether you think the suspect is guilty or innocent. Let's say that 63 percent of people think the defendant is guilty.*

Now imagine the same thing happens with a slight twist. This time the prosecution is allowed to tell a story, and the defense can only use witnesses to refute the claims. The same facts are revealed; it is just the format of the information that changes. The prosecution lays out the facts in a neat story order, but the defense must rely upon the facts randomly popping up as the witnesses testify. In a rational world, this obviously won't matter. However, guess the percentage of people who said the defendant was guilty this time around—a staggering 78 percent!

Okay, now let's reverse the roles. Now the defense can tell a story, but the prosecution must rely upon witnesses to build their case. Any guesses as to the percentage of jurors who thought the defendant was guilty under this

*N. Pennington and R. Hastie, "Explanation-Based Decision Making," *Journal of Experimental Psychology: Learning, Memory and Cognition* 14 (1988): 521–533.

treatment? A lowly 31 percent. This clearly demonstrates the power that stories have over us: a near 50 percentage point swing in the number of people saying someone is guilty of first degree murder based on whether a story was told or not.

Another frightening example comes from the realm of medicine.* This time participants were given information on the effectiveness of treatments as a percentage of those cured overall (ranging from 90 to 30 percent). This is known as base rate information. They were also given a story, which could be positive, negative. or ambiguous.

For instance, the positive story read as follows: Pat's decision to undergo Tamoxol resulted in a positive outcome. The entire worm was destroyed. Doctors were confident the disease would not resume its course. At one-month post-treatment, Pat's recovery was certain.

The negative story read: Pat's decision to undergo Tamoxol resulted in a poor outcome. The worm was not completely destroyed. The disease resumed its course. At 1-month post-treatment, Pat was blind and had lost the ability to walk.

Subjects were then asked would they undergo the treatment if they were diagnosed with the disease. Of course,

*A. Freymuth and G. Ronan, "Modeling Patient Decision-Making: The Role of Base-Rate and Anecdotal Information," *Journal of Clinical Psychology in Medical Settings* 11 (2004): 211–216.

people should have relied upon the base rate information of the effectiveness of treatment as it represented a full sample of experience. But did this actually happen?

Of course not. Instead the base rate information was essentially ignored in favor of the anecdotal story. For instance, when participants were given a positive story and were told the treatment was 90 percent effective, 88 percent of people thought they would go with the treatment. However, when the participants were given a negative story and again told the treatment was 90 percent effective, only 39 percent of people opted to pursue this line of treatment.

Conversely, when told the treatment was only 30 percent effective and given a negative story, only 7 percent said they would follow this treatment. However, when low effectiveness was combined with a good story, 78 percent of people said they would take the drug. As you can see, the evidence on effectiveness of the treatments was completely ignored in favor of the power of the story.

Somewhat strangely perhaps, price may even act as a story in its own right. For instance, which works betters—a painkiller than costs $2.50 per dose, or the same painkiller discounted and selling at just 10 cents?*

*R.L. Waber, B. Shiv, and D. Ariely, "Commercial Features of Placebo and Therapeutic Efficacy," *Journal of the American Medical Association* 299 (2008): 1016–1017.

Rationally, of course, they should have exactly the same effect (especially since both pills were nothing more than sugar pills). However, as you have no doubt guessed, the pills had very different reported effects. Some 85 percent of people reported less pain when they thought the drug had cost the higher price of $2.50. However, only 61 percent said the painkiller was effective when they thought it cost 10 cents.

If you prefer booze to pills, then consider the following story of price.* Let's imagine you are given some wine to taste and told it costs $10 a bottle, and then some more wine and told that this second one costs $90 a bottle. Most people who found themselves in this enviable position said the $90 wine tasted nearly twice as good as the $10 wine. The only snag is that the $10 wine and the $90 wine were exactly the same wine! People were simply misled by the price.

Stock Market Stories

Could something similar be at work in the stock market? It is possible that investors shun value stocks because of their poor stories and low prices. As Joel Greenblatt has observed, one of the reasons people shy away from

*H. Plassmann, J. O'Doherty, B. Shiv. and A. Rangel, "Marketing Actions Can Modulate Neural Representations of Experienced Utility," *Proceedings of the National Academy of Science* 105:3 (2008): 1050–1054.

value investing is that the stocks you consider have poor stories. As he puts it "The companies that show up on the screens can be scary and not doing so well, so people find them difficult to buy." Support for this view comes from researchers* who have explored the characteristics and performance of the most "Admired" and "Despised" stocks from Fortune magazine's annual survey.

The most-admired companies tend to be those that have done well in the past, in both stock market and financial performance. They also tend to be relatively expensive. For instance, the average sales growth for a company in the most-admired list is 10 percent per year over the last two years. In contrast, the despised stocks seem to have been disasters, with an average sales growth of just 3.5 percent. Thus the admired stocks have great stories and high prices attached to them, whereas the despised stocks have terrible stories and sport low valuations.

Which would you rather own? Psychologically, we know you will feel attracted to the admired stocks. Yet, the despised stocks are generally a far better investment. They significantly outperform the market as well as the admired stocks.

At the other end of the spectrum from value stocks is another group of stocks that have very different stories

*M. Statman, K. Fisher, and D. Anginer, "Affect in a Behavioral Asset Pricing Model," unpublished paper.

attached to them. I'm talking about initial public offerings. IPOs are companies that have come to the market for the first time to offer their stock to the public. Such stocks generally have great stories attached to them.

One prime example that captured investors' imaginations was an online gaming company. The stock had a great story—online was still sexy, and gambling was sexy squared. Everyone was exceedingly excited about the growth prospects for this firm. Investors simply couldn't get enough of the stock; the IPO was 14 times oversubscribed. However, investors significantly overpaid for the stock. There was simply no margin of safety for purchases. So, when the firm missed their earning report just six months after listing, its price halved, much to the chagrin of the investors.

Sadly, this isn't an isolated case. IPOs always seem to entice investors to part with their cash. However, IPOs are in general truly terrible investments. For instance, in the United States the average IPO has underperformed the market by 21 percent per annum in the three years after its listing (covering the period 1980-2007). Similar patterns can be found in most countries.

One study used the methodology we outlined in Chapter 6 to investigate the potential source of this appalling performance.* They reverse engineered the price at which

*G.M. Cogliati , S. Paleari , and S. Vismara, "IPO Pricing: Growth Rates Implied in Offer Prices" (2008), unpublished paper.

the stock came to market, in order to try and find the implied cash flow growth rate that investors thought these stocks had. The average price implied 33 percent yearly growth. What did these stocks actually manage to deliver? Nothing short of a disaster. The average delivered free cash flow growth was −55 percent over five years—talk about overpaying for the hope of growth!

Despite the fact that long-term IPO underperformance is a very well documented fact, investors keep stepping up to the plate and purchasing IPOs. I suspect this is because the stories overwhelm the evidence, just as occurred in the medical study outlined above.

Beware of Capitalizing Hope

The problem of overpaying for the hope of growth isn't unique to IPOs. Ben Graham warned of the dangers inherent in "The capitalization of entirely conjectural future prospects," or what today might well be described as the capitalization of hope. I suspect it is the most common mistake that I encounter when talking to investors.

Rob Arnott and colleagues have found that investors nearly always overpay for the hope of growth.* They take

*R.D. Arnott, F. Li, and K.F. Sherrerd, "Clairvoyant Value and the Growth-Value Cycle, "*Journal of Portfolio Management* 35 (Summer 2009): 142–157 and "Clairvoyant Value and the Value Effect," *Journal of Portfolio Management* 35 (Spring 2009): 12–26.

a novel approach to assessing the problem. Starting at the price of a stock way back in 1956, they compare this price to the actual delivered cash returns to investors (essentially the dividends and repurchases) over the next 50 years. This is an example of what is called perfect foresight. It imagines that we knew exactly what the future was going to hold, what price should we have paid given the returns achieved?

As Arnott notes:

> The market *never failed to overpay* for the long-term realized successes of the growth companies, even though the market chose *which* companies deserved the premium multiples with remarkable accuracy. . . . Nearly half of the price-implied relative growth expectations of the growth and value stocks failed to materialize, so investors were paying twice the fair premium for growth stocks relative to value.

Let me give you an example of the dangers of simple stories from the recent investing past. Although I could have selected from many examples, such as emerging markets decoupling, I've settled on the mining sector for the purposes of illustration.

The simple story during the period 2003–2008 was that China would grow to the sky. Stories along the lines of "Chinese demand is revolutionizing global commodity markets; China has already overtaken the USA as the largest consumer of iron ore, steel, and copper; the China effect seems unstoppable" were commonplace. As is often the case, there is no doubt a kernel of truth contained within the simple story. But this shouldn't be the basis of an investment. Nonetheless, the mining sector caught the China bug, and talk of a mining "super cycle" was rife.

Based on these stories, let's see how the analysts reacted to the situation. Exhibit 10.1 shows the earnings per share for the global mining sector. You can see the massive surge in earnings that occurred in the period

EXHIBIT 10.1   World Mining Sector Earnings and Forecasts

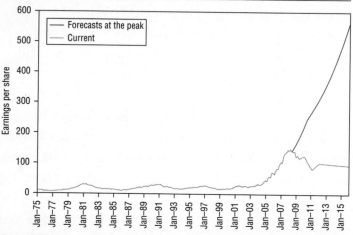

Source: GMO.

from 2003–2007. Now faced with such a surge, you might have thought the analysts would predict some kind of reversion to the mean. But no, instead they pumped up the super cycle, drank the purple KoolAid and proclaimed "This time is different." Far from predicting a return to more normal times, the analysts predicted that the growth we had witnessed was just the beginning of something truly extraordinary. The analysts were forecasting 12.5 percent growth annually for the foreseeable future. This was pretty much double the rate than had been achieved historically.

Of course, the analysts were completely wrong, as were the investors who had been following them blindly. Instead of a massive super cycle, the world faced the largest downturn since the Great Depression. This isn't just obvious with the benefit of hindsight. The straight line extrapolation of growth forecasts is a classic sign of trouble ahead in real time.

Focus on the Facts

So, what can we do to guard against the siren song of stories? The answer is relatively simple: We must focus on the facts—as Dragnet fans will recall, "Just the facts." Stories usually have an emotional content, hence they appeal to the X-system—the quick and dirty way of thinking. If you want to use the more logical system of thought (the C-system), then you must focus on the facts. Generally, facts are emotionally cold, and thus will pass from the X-system to the C-system.

Ben Graham insisted that "safety must be based on study and standards," and that valuations be "justified by the facts, e.g., the assets, earnings, dividends, definite prospects, as distinct, let us say, from market quotations established by artificial manipulation or distorted by psychological excesses." These wise words ring as true today as when Graham wrote them way back in 1934, but very few investors seem capable of heeding them. Focusing on the cold hard facts (soundly based in real numbers) is likely to be our best defense against the siren song of stories.

Chapter Eleven

This Time Is Different

~

Your Biggest Advantage over the Pros

Pᴇʀʜᴀᴘs ᴛʜᴇ ᴍᴏsᴛ ᴏʙᴠɪᴏᴜs ᴀʀᴇᴀ of contact that the public will have with behavioral finance, and certainly the most high profile, is the occurrence of bubbles. According to most standard models of finance, bubbles shouldn't really exist. Yet they have been with us pretty much since time immemorial. The first stock exchange was founded in 1602. The first equity bubble occurred just 118 years later—the South Sea Bubble. Before that, of course, was the Tulipmania of 1637.

At GMO we define a bubble as a (real) price movement that is at least two standard deviations from trend. Now, if market returns were normally distributed as predicted by the efficient markets hypothesis, a two standard deviation event should occur roughly every 44 years. However, we found a staggering 30 plus bubbles since 1925—that is the equivalent of slightly more than one every three years. Not only did we find such a large number of bubbles, but every single one of the them burst, taking us back down two standard deviations. That should happen once every 2,000 years, not 30 times in 84 years! This is the elephant in the room for those who believe in efficient markets.

There is also a view that bubbles are somehow "black swans." Taleb defined a black swan as a highly improbable event with three principal characteristics:

1. It is unpredictable.
2. It has massive impact.
3. Ex-post, explanations are concocted that make the event appear less random and more predictable than it was.

It would be terribly reassuring if bubbles were black swans; then we would be absolved from our behavior.

However, such a defense is largely an abdication of responsibility. The belief that bubbles are black swans has found support at the highest levels. Both Alan Greenspan and Ben Bernanke have been keen proponents of this view as they continually argued that it was impossible to diagnose a bubble before it burst, and hence argued that the best a central bank can do is try and mop up after everything goes wrong.

Why Can't We Time Predictable Surprises?

This is, of course, utter rubbish. It is an attempt to abdicate responsibility. Bubbles and their bursts aren't black swans. They are "predictable surprises."* This may sound like an oxymoron, but it isn't. Predictable surprises also have three defining characteristics:

1. At least some people are aware of the problem.
2. The problem gets worse over time.
3. Eventually the problem explodes into a crisis, much to the shock of most.

The problem with predictable surprises is that while there is little uncertainty that a large disaster awaits, there is considerable uncertainty over the timing of that disaster.

*M. Bazerman and M. Watkins, *Predictable Surprises: The Disasters You Should Have Seen Coming and How to Prevent Them* (Cambridge, MA: Harvard Business Press, 2004).

Take the credit crisis of 2007/8, which has been described by Jeremy Grantham as the most widely predicted crisis of all time. Cacophonies of Cassandras were queuing up to warn of the dangers—even some of the Federal Reserve governors were warning of the problems of lax lending standards. Robert Shiller reissued his book, *Irrational Exuberance*, in 2005 with a new chapter dedicated to the housing market. Even I (sitting on the other side of the Atlantic) wrote a paper in 2005 arguing that the U.S. housing market showed all the classic hallmarks of a mania.

This discussion of people warning of the danger of the credit bubble might seem odd coming just a few chapters after my rant on the folly of forecasting. However, I think a clear line can be drawn between analysis and forecasting. As Ben Graham put it, "Analysis connotes the careful study of available facts with the attempt to draw conclusions therefrom based on established principles and sound logic."

So the big question is: What prevents us from seeing these predictable surprises? At least five major psychological hurdles hamper us. Some of these barriers we have already encountered. Firstly, there is our old friend, *overoptimism*. Everyone simply believes that they are less likely than average to have a drinking problem, to get divorced, or to be fired. This tendency to look on the bright side helps to blind us to the dangers posed by predictable surprises.

In addition to our over-optimism, we suffer from the *illusion of control*—the belief that we can influence the outcome of uncontrollable events. This is where we encounter a lot of the pseudoscience of finance, things like Value-at-Risk (VaR). The idea that if we can quantify risk then we can control it is one of the great fallacies of modern finance. VaR tells us how much you can expect to lose with a given probability, such as the maximum daily loss with a 95 percent probability. Such risk management techniques are akin to buying a car with an airbag that is guaranteed to work unless you crash. But as we saw earlier, simply providing a number can make people feel safer—the illusion of safety.

We have also encountered the third hurdle to spotting predictable surprises. It is *self-serving bias*—the innate desire to interpret information and act in ways that are supportive of our own self-interests. The Warren Buffett quotation we used earlier is apposite once again and bears repeating: "Never ask a barber if you need a haircut." If you had been a risk manager in 2006 suggesting that some of the collateralized debt obligations (CDOs) that your bank was working on might have been slightly suspect, you would, of course, have been fired and replaced by a risk manager who was happy to approve the transaction. Whenever lots of people are making lots of money, it is unlikely that they will take a step back and point out the obvious flaws in their actions.

The dot-com bubble in the late 1990s revealed some prime examples of self-serving bias at work. The poster child for poor behavior was Henry Blodget, then of Merrill Lynch. The scale of his hypocrisy was really quite breathtaking. At the same time as he was telling clients in a research report that "We don't see much downside to the shares," he was writing internally that the stock was "such a piece of crap!" He also wrote, "We think LFMN presents an attractive investment" in a report while simultaneously writing, "I can't believe what a POS (piece of shit) that thing is" internally! Of course, Blodget wasn't alone (think Jack Grubman and the likes of Mary Meeker); he was just a particularly egregious example.

The penultimate hurdle is *myopia*—an overt focus on the short term. All too often we find that consequences that occur at a later date tend to have much less bearing on our choices the further into the future they fall. This can be summed up as "Eat, drink, and be merry, for tomorrow we may die." Of course, this ignores the fact that on any given day we are roughly 260,000 times more likely to be wrong than right with respect to making it to tomorrow. Myopia can be summed up via Saint Augustine's plea, "Lord, make me chaste, but not yet"—one more good year, one more good bonus, and then I promise to go and do something worthwhile with my life, rather than working in finance!

The final barrier to spotting predictable surprises is a form of *inattentional blindness*. Put bluntly, we simply don't expect to see what we are not looking for. The classic experiment in this field* shows a short video clip of two teams playing basketball. One team is dressed in white, the other dressed in black. You are asked to count how many times the team in white passed the basketball between themselves. Now half way through this clip a man in a gorilla suit walks on and beats his chest and then walks off. At the end of the clip, you are asked how many passes there were, and the normal range of answers is somewhere between 14 and 17. You are then asked if you saw anything unusual. About 60 percent of people fail to spot the gorilla! When the researcher points out the gorilla, and re-runs the tape, people always say you switched the clip, and the gorilla wasn't there in the first version. Basically, this study demonstrates that people get too caught up in the detail of trying to count the passes. I suspect that something similar happens in finance; investors get caught up in all the details and the noise, and forget to keep an eye on the big picture.

*D.J. Simons and C.F. Chabris, "Gorillas in Our Midst: Sustained Inattentional Blindness for Dynamic Events," *Perception* 28 (1999): 1059–1074.

A Beginner's Guide to Spotting Bubbles

So what can we do to improve this sorry state of affairs? Essentially, we must remember Herb Stein's prosaic and prophetic words of wisdom: "If something can't go on forever, it won't." This is a deceptively simple and yet immensely insightful phrase. If markets seem too good to be true, they probably are. Learning to remember this simple fact would help prevent a great deal of the angst caused when the bubble bursts.

A good working knowledge of the history of bubbles can also help preserve your capital. Ben Graham argued that an investor should "have an adequate idea of stock market history, in terms particularly of the major fluctuations. With this background he may be in a position to form some worthwhile judgment of the attractiveness or dangers . . . of the market." Nowhere is an appreciation of history more important than in understanding bubbles.

Although the details of bubbles change, the underlying patterns and dynamics are eerily similar. The framework I have long used to think about bubbles has its roots way back in 1867, in a paper written by John Stuart Mill.* Mill was a quite extraordinary man, a polymath and a polyglot, a philosopher, a poet, an economist, and a Member

---

*John Stuart Mill, "On Credit Cycles and the Origin of Commercial Panics," *Manchester Statistical Society* (1867): 11–40.

of Parliament. He was distinctly enlightened in matters of social justice, penning papers which were anti-slavery and pro extended suffrage. From our narrow perspective, it is his work on understanding the patterns of bubbles that is most useful. As Mill put it, "The malady of commercial crisis is not, in essence, a matter of the purse but of the mind."

His model has been used time and again, and forms the basis of the bubble framework utilized by such luminaries as Hyman Minsky, one of the few economists worth listening to, and Charles Kindleberger, the preeminent chronicler of financial manias. Essentially this model breaks a bubble's rise and fall into five phases as shown below.

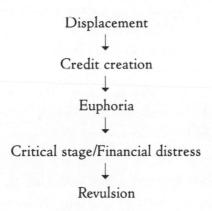

Displacement
↓
Credit creation
↓
Euphoria
↓
Critical stage/Financial distress
↓
Revulsion

Displacement—The birth of a boom. Displacement is generally an exogenous shock that triggers the creation of profit opportunities in some sectors, while closing down profit availability in other sectors. As long as the opportunities created are greater than those that get shut down, investment and production will pick up to exploit these new opportunities. Investment in both financial and physical assets is likely to occur. Effectively, we are witnessing the birth of a boom. As Mill puts it, "A new confidence begins to germinate early in this period, but its growth is slow."

Credit creation—The nurturing of a bubble. Just as fire can't grow without oxygen, so a boom needs credit to feed on. Minsky argued that monetary expansion and credit creation are largely endogenous to the system. That is to say, not only can money be created by existing banks but also by the formation of new banks, the development of new credit instruments, and the expansion of personal credit outside the banking system. Mill noted that during this phase "The rate of interest [is] almost uniformly low. . . . Credit . . . continues to grow more robust, enterprise to increase and profits to enlarge."

Euphoria—Everyone starts to buy into the new era. Prices are seen as only capable of always going up. Traditional valuation standards are abandoned, and new measures are introduced to justify the current price.

A wave of over-optimism and overconfidence is unleashed, leading people to overestimate the gains, underestimate the risks, and generally think they can control the situation. The new era dominates discussions, and Sir John Templeton's four most dangerous words in investing, "This time is different," reverberate around the market.

As Mill wrote, "There is a morbid excess of belief . . . healthy confidence . . . has degenerated into the disease of a too facile faith. . . . The crowd of . . . investors . . . do not, in their excited mood, think of the pertinent questions, whether their capital will become quickly productive, and whether their commitment is out of proportion to their means. . . . Unfortunately, however, in the absence of adequate foresight and self-control, the tendency is for speculation to attain its most rapid growth exactly when its growth is most dangerous."

Critical stage—Financial distress. This leads to the critical stage that is often characterized by insiders cashing out, and is rapidly followed by financial distress, in which the excess leverage that has been built up during the boom becomes a major problem. Fraud also often emerges during this stage of the bubble's life.

Mill was aware of the dangers that the use of leverage posed and how it could easily result in asset fire sales. "The . . . trader who employs, in addition to his own means, a proportion of borrowed Capital . . . has found, in the moment of crisis, the conjuring power of his name utterly vanished, and has been compelled to provide for inexorably maturing obligations by the forced sales of goods or produce at such prices as would tempt forth reluctant capital."

Final Stage—Revulsion. The final stage of a bubble's life cycle is revulsion. Investors are so scarred by the events in which they participated that they can no longer bring themselves to participate in the market at all. This results in bargain basement asset prices.

Mill opined, "As a rule, Panics do not destroy capital; they merely reveal the extent to which it has been previously destroyed by its betrayal into hopelessly unproductive works. . . . The failure of great banks . . . and mercantile firms . . . are the symptoms incident to the disease, not the disease itself."

Mill was also aware of the prolonged nature of a recovery in the wake of a bubble: "Economy, enforced on great numbers of people by losses from failures and from depreciated investments restricts their purchasing power. . . . Profits are kept down to the stunted proportions of demand. . . . Time alone can steady the shattered nerves, and form a healthy cicatrice over wounds so deep."

Pretty much every bubble in history can be mapped against this framework. It should help to guide us in our thinking and analysis when it comes to avoiding bubbles.

Your Edge Over the Pros!

Believe it or not, you actually have one huge edge over the professionals when trying to overcome this pitfall: You don't have to be a slave to an arbitrary benchmark.

As Keynes observed, "It is the long-term investor, he who most promotes the public interest, who will in practice come in for most criticism, wherever investment funds are managed by committees or boards or banks. For it is in the essence of his behavior that he should be eccentric, unconventional and rash in the eyes of average opinion. If he is successful, that will only confirm the general belief in his rashness; and if in the short run he is unsuccessful, which is very likely, he will not receive much mercy."

According to classical finance, bubbles should be prevented by the presence of arbitrageurs. These guys sit around waiting for opportunities to exploit the herd and drive prices back towards some form of equilibrium. Sadly, not many professional investors actually do this.

Those few who do try to stand against bubbles must avoid the use of leverage. As Mill noted above, those who try to fulfill this role while using leverage often find themselves coming to a sticky end (witness the end of LTCM in 1998). As Keynes said, "The market may remain irrational, longer than you can remain solvent."

Yet, another group of professionals actually chooses to become bubble riders. They amplify rather than reduce the bubble—confident in their abilities to exit at the top or very close to it. Hoare's Bank did exactly this during the South Sea Bubble of 1720, and some hedge funds played a similar role during the dot.com mania.*

However, the vast majority of professional investors simply don't try to arbitrage against bubbles because of self-serving bias and myopia. They are benchmarked against an index and fear underperforming that index above all else (aka career risk); thus they don't have the appetite to stand against bubbles. This is amplified by the fact that most fund management organizations are paid on the basis of assets under management, so the easiest way of not getting fired is to deliver a performance close to the benchmark (aka business risk). These two elements of self-serving bias collude to prevent many managers from "doing the right thing."

---

*P. Temin and H. Voth, "Riding the South Sea Bubble" (Unpublished paper); and M. Brunnermeier and S. Nagel, "Hedge Funds and the Technology Bubble," *Journal of Finance* 59 (2004): 2013–2040.

Of course thankfully there are exceptions. Jean Marie Eveillard of First Eagle has said "I would rather lose half my clients, than half my client's money." Similarly, Jeremy Grantham's refusal to participate in the dot.com bubble cost him about two-thirds of his asset allocation book. Such a willingness to take on career and business risk is, sadly, a very rare commodity indeed. However, as an individual investor you don't have to worry about career or business risk. This is your greatest advantage over the professionals.

Investors should remember bubbles are a by-product of human behavior, and human behavior is all too predictable. The details of each bubble are subtly different, but the general patterns remain eerily similar. As such, bubbles and their bursts are clearly not black swans. Of course, the timing of the eventual bursting of the bubble remains as uncertain as ever, but the patterns of the events themselves are all too predictable. As Jean Marie Eveillard observed, "Sometimes, what matters is not so much how low the odds are that circumstances would turn negative, what matters more is what the consequences would be if that happens." In other words, sometimes the potentially long term negative outcomes are so severe that investors simply can't afford to ignore them, even in the short term.

Chapter Twelve

Right for the Wrong Reason, or Wrong for the Right Reason

***

Writing Away Your Mistakes and Biases

IN THE LAST CHAPTER WE SAW THAT BUBBLES follow very similar paths, although the details vary over time. This raises the very important question, why don't we learn from our mistakes? The historic financial landscape is peppered with examples of bubbles, from the South Sea Bubble of the 1700s, to the Japanese bubble in the late

1980s, the dot-com bubble at the turn of the this century, and of course, the current credit/housing bubble. You might have thought that we humans might have learnt from history. However, yet another pitfall of the X-system is an unwillingness to recognize our mistakes and errors as such. Instead we gloss over them.

John Kenneth Galbraith, an unusually insightful economist, said the markets are characterized by:

> . . . extreme brevity of the financial memory. In consequence, financial disaster is quickly forgotten. In further consequence, when the same or closely similar circumstances occur again, sometimes in a few years, they are hailed by a new, often youthful, and always supremely self-confident generation as a brilliantly innovative discovery in the financial and larger economic world. There can be few fields of human endeavor in which history counts for so little as in the world of finance.

My favorite quotation on the lack of historical appreciation in finance comes from Jeremy Grantham, the chief strategist at GMO (we met him in Chapter 2 and again in Chapter 11) who, when asked, "Do you think we will learn anything from this turmoil?" responded, "We will learn an enormous amount in the very short term, quite a bit in the medium term, and absolutely nothing in the long term. That would be the historical precedent."

Of course, in order to learn from a mistake, we need to understand that it is a mistake. This may sound obvious but we have to overcome at least two psychological biases—self-attribution bias and hindsight bias.

It's Not My Fault, It's Just Bad Luck

Self-attribution bias is our habit of attributing good outcomes to our skill as investors, while blaming bad outcomes on something or somebody else.

Sports events are a great example of this kind of thinking. For instance, psychologists* looked at the explanations offered in the sports pages to study the presence of attribution bias among athletes. In evaluating an athlete/coach's opinion of his performance, they ask themselves if the performance was due to an internal factor (i.e., something relative to the team's abilities) or an external factor (such as a bad referee). Unsurprisingly, self-attribution was present. Seventy-five percent of the time following a win, an internal attribution was made (the result of skill), whereas only 55 percent of the time following a loss was an internal attribution made.

*R. Lau and D. Russell, "Attributions in the Sports Pages," *Journal of Personality and Social Psychology* 39 (1980): 29–38.

The bias was even more evident when the explanations were further categorized as coming from either a player/coach or a sportswriter. Players and coaches attributed their success to an internal factor more than 80 percent of the time. However, internal factors were blamed only 53 percent of the time following losses.

The same thing happens when it comes to investing. It is all too easy for investors to dismiss poor results as examples of bad luck. On some occasions this may well be the case, but on others bad analysis may be the root cause.

In a recent speech, David Einhorn of Greenlight Capital pointed out, "When something goes wrong, I like to think about the bad decisions and learn from them so that hopefully I don't repeat the same mistake." He goes on to provide an example of a mistake he once made. In 2005 he recommended buying MDC holdings, a homebuilder, at $67 per share. In the following four years, MDC dropped about 40 percent. As Einhorn stated, "The loss was not bad luck; it was bad analysis." Simply put, he failed to understand the importance of the big picture, in this case the U.S. housing and credit bubble.

Sadly, few of us are as introspective as Einhorn. So to combat the pervasive problem of self-attribution we really need to keep a written record of the decisions we take and the reasons behind those decisions—an investment diary, if you will. Keeping an investment diary may sound daft, but George Soros did exactly that. In his *Alchemy of Finance* he writes "I kept a diary in which I recorded the thoughts that went into my investment decisions on a real-time basis. . . . The experiment was a roaring success in financial terms—my fund never did better. It also produced a surprising result: I came out of the experiment with quite different expectations about the future."

Having kept such a diary, we then need to map the outcomes of the decisions and the reasons behind those decisions into a quadrant diagram, like the one shown below. That is, was I right for the right reason? (I can claim some skill, it could still be luck, but at least I can claim skill), or was I right for some spurious reason? (In which case I will keep the result because it makes the portfolio look good, but I shouldn't fool myself into thinking that I really knew what I was doing.) Was I wrong for the wrong reason? (I made a mistake and I need to learn from it), or was I wrong for the right reason? (After all, bad luck does occur and price volatility dwarfs fundamental volatility in our world.)

Only by cross-referencing our decisions and the reasons for those decisions with the outcomes, can we hope to understand when we are lucky and when we have used genuine skill, and more importantly, where we are making persistent recurrent mistakes.

	Good Outcome	Bad Outcome
Right reasoning	Skill (perhaps)	Bad luck
Wrong reasoning	Good luck	Mistake

Don't Be a Monday Morning Quarterback

One of the reasons I suggest that people keep a written record of their decisions and the reasons behind their decisions, is that if they don't, they run the risk of suffering from the second bias that prevents us from learning from our investment mistakes: hindsight bias. This simply refers to the idea that once we know the outcome we tend to think we knew it all the time.

In finance, we seem to enjoy an Orwellian rewriting of history after each bubble. In the wake of each bubble a deluge of texts appears telling us what went wrong and why, usually penned by those who hadn't spotted the problem in the first place. This is a form of the ex-post rationalization that makes events seem much more predictable than they were beforehand.

Psychologists* have shown that this tendency crops up with alarming regularity. For instance, in one experiment

*B. Fischhoff, "Hindsight ≠ Foresight: The Effect of Outcome Knowledge on Judgment under Uncertainty," *Journal of Experimental Psychology: Human Perception and Performance* 1 (1975): 288–299.

students were given descriptions of the British occupation of India and problems of the Gurkas of Nepal. The information provided went along the following lines: In 1814, Hastings (the governor-general) decided that he had to deal with the Gurkas once and for all. The campaign was far from glorious and the troops suffered in the extreme conditions. The Gurkas were skilled at guerrilla style warfare, and as they were few in number, there was little chance for full-scale engagements. The British learned caution only after several defeats.

Having read a much longer version of the above, the students were told to assign probabilities to each of the four following outcomes:

1. British victory
2. Gurka victory
3. Military stalemate without a peace settlement
4. Military stalemate with a peace settlement

Another group of students read the same thing, but this group was provided with the "true" outcome. The only snag was that each of four outcomes was labeled the true outcome. So some students were told outcome one was really the result and others were told outcome two was the result, and so on.

Strangely enough, when people were told the supposed true outcome they upped the probability they attached to that outcome. In fact, they nearly doubled the probability they placed on the outcome compared to the group who weren't given any information on the outcomes. That is to say, people weren't capable of ignoring the ex-post outcome in their decision-making.

This study demonstrates why a real-time investment diary can be a very real benefit to investors because it helps to hold us true to our thoughts at the actual point in time, rather than our reassessed version of events after we know the outcomes. An investment diary is a simple but very effective method of learning from mistakes, and should form a central part of your approach to investment.

The Perils of ADHD Investing

Never Underestimate the Value of Doing Nothing

WE HAVE LEARNED IN THIS BOOK that one of the barriers that prevents a lot of investors from acting against bubbles is myopia, an overt focus on the short term. However, this tendency to think short-term isn't unique to bubbles. We see it all the time. Investors today appear to have chronic attention deficit hyperactivity disorder (ADHD) when it comes to their portfolio.

Exhibit 13.1 illustrates the problem. It shows the average holding period for a stock on the New York Stock Exchange (NYSE). Today the average holding period is around six months! In the 1950s and 1960s investors used to hold stocks for seven or eight years—interestingly, this was before the rise of the institutional investment as we know it today. Of course, if you hold a stock for just six months, you don't care at all about the long term, you simply care about the next couple of quarterly earnings figures.

This focus on the short term is hard to reconcile with any fundamental view of investing. We can examine the drivers of equity returns to see what we need to understand in order to invest. At a one-year time horizon, the

EXHIBIT 13.1   The Average Holding Period for a Stock on the NYSE (years)

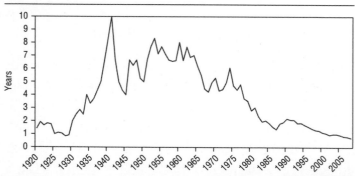

Source: GMO.

vast majority of your total return comes from changes in valuation—which are effectively random fluctuations in price. However, at a five-year time horizon, 80 percent of your total return is generated by the price you pay for the investment plus the growth in the underlying cash flow. These are the aspects of investment that fundamental investors should understand, and they clearly only matter in the long term.

Sadly, as Keynes appositely observed, "Human nature desires quick results, there is a peculiar zest in making money quickly . . . compared with their predecessors, modern investors concentrate too much on annual, quarterly and even monthly valuations of what they hold, and on capital appreciation." Regrettably, the quarters and months that Keynes alluded to have become days and minutes for some investors today.

What Can We Learn from Goalkeepers?

Not only do we desire quick results but we love to be seen as doing something (as opposed to doing nothing); we have a distinct bias towards action. Soccer goal keepers provide us with a great example of this unfortunate tendency. For the record, despite the stereotypical image of the British being obsessed with soccer, I know very little about the game. Since I grew up playing rugby all winter and cricket all summer, our so-called national game leaves me cold.

Nevertheless, we can learn from the experience of the goalkeepers. Although not normally the stars of the team, it transpires that when it comes to penalty kicks top goalkeepers are action men. A recent study* revealed some fascinating patterns when it comes to trying to save penalties. In soccer, when a penalty is awarded, the ball is placed 11 meters from the goal, and it is a simple contest between the goalkeeper and the kicker. The goalkeeper may not move from his line until the kick has occurred.

Given that in the average soccer match 2.5 goals are scored, a penalty (which has an 80 percent chance of resulting in a goal) can dramatically influence the result of the game. So, unlike in many psychological experiments, the stakes are significant.

Our intrepid researchers examined some 311 penalty kicks from top leagues and championships worldwide. A panel of three independent judges was used to analyze the direction of the kick and the direction of movement by the goalkeeper. To avoid confusion, all directions (left or right) were relayed from the goalkeeper's perspective.

Very roughly speaking, the kicks were equally distributed with about one third of the kicks aimed at the left, center, and right of the goal mouth. However, the keepers

*M. Bar-eli, O. Azar, I. Ritov, Y. Keidar-Levin, and G. Schein, "Action Bias among Elite Soccer Goalkeepers: The Case of Penalty Kicks" (Unpublished paper, 2005).

displayed a distinct action bias: They either dived left or right (94 percent of the time), hardly ever choosing to remain in the center of their goal.

Yet, they would have been much more successful if they had just stood in the center of the goal. According to the stats, when the goalkeeper stays in the center of the goal he saves some 60 percent of the kicks aimed at the center, far higher than his saving rate when he dives either left or right. However, goalkeepers stay in the center only 6 percent of the time.

The goalkeepers were asked why they choose to dive rather than stand in the center. The defense offered was that at least they feel they are making an effort when they dive left or right, whereas standing in the center and watching a goal scored to the left or the right of you would feel much worse. Well, I don't know about you, but in my opinion, nothing could be worse than losing, regardless of where you stand.

Poor Performance Increases the Desire to Act

One final aspect of the bias to action is especially note-worthy—the urge to act tends to intensify after a loss—a period of poor performance, in portfolio terms. Psychologists*

*M. Zeelenberg, K. Van Den Bos, E. Van Dijk, and R/ Pieters, "The Inaction Effect in the Psychology of Regret," *Journal of Personality and Social Psychology* 62 (2002): 314–327.

have asked people to consider something like the following scenario.

Steenland and Straathof are both coaches of soccer teams. Steenland is the coach of Blue-Black, and Straathof is the coach of E.D.O. Both coaches lost their prior game with a score of 4-0. This Sunday, Steenland decides to do something: he fields three new players. Straathof decides not to change his team. This time both teams lose with a score line of 3-0. Who feels more regret, coach Steenland or coach Straathof?

Participants saw this statement in one of three forms. Some saw it as presented above—framed in terms of a prior loss; others were simply given the second half of the above with no information on prior events; and the final group saw a version in which both coaches had won the previous week but lost this week.

If the teams had won last week, then 90 percent of the respondents thought the coach making changes would feel more regret when the team lost this week. However, when the situation is presented as the teams losing both weeks, the coach not taking any action was thought to be feeling more regret by nearly 70 percent of respondents. The logic was that "if only" the coach had made some changes, he might not have lost for a second week in a row. This highlights the role that counterfactual thinking plays in our judgments. When dealing with losses, the urge to reach for an action bias is exceptionally high.

Investors and Action Bias

In order to introduce you to the evidence of an action bias among investors I must first introduce the field of laboratory experiments in economics, specifically experimental asset markets. These are great contraptions for investigating how people behave in a financial market context without any complicating factors.

In these experiments, markets are very simple consisting of just one asset and cash. The asset is a share, which pays out a dividend once per period. The dividend paid depends upon the state of the world (four possible states). Each state is equally weighted (i.e., there is a 25 percent probability of each state occurring in any given period).

Once you know the various payouts in each state of the world, it is trivial to calculate the expected value (simply the payoffs multiplied by their probabilities, then multiplied by the number of time periods remaining). The fundamental value of such an asset clearly decreases over time by the amount of the expected dividend paid out in each period. Now you might think that this was a simple asset to trade. However, the evidence suggests otherwise.

EXHIBIT 13.2   Results from Asset Markets

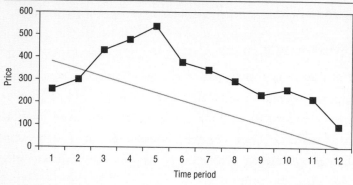

Source: Lei et al. (2001).

Exhibit 13.2 shows a typical result from one of these asset markets. The asset starts off significantly under-valued, and then rises massively above fair value, before crashing back to fundamental value in the final periods.

This is nothing more than a simple bubble forming and bursting. So what has this got to do with action bias? Well, the exhibit comes from a particularly interesting version of the experimental asset market.* In this particular version of the game, once you had bought shares you were prohibited from reselling them. This rules out the possibility of a greater fool theory driving the bubble.

*V. Lei, C. Moussair, and C. Plott, "Nonspeculative Bubbles in Experimental Asset Markets: Lack of Common Knowledge of Rationality vs. Actual Irrationality," *Econometrica* 69 (2001): 831–859.

That is to say, because you can't resell the shares, there is no point in buying them above fair value in the hope you can sell them onto someone else for even more gain. In effect, participants were simply trading out of boredom! So it appears that investors have a bias to action as well.

Waiting for the Fat Pitch

The antithesis of this action bias is, of course, patience. Patience is a weapon you can use to protect yourself from becoming an ADHD investor. It is required because the curse of the value investor is to be too early—both in terms of buying (known affectionately as premature accumulation) and in terms of selling. Unfortunately, in the short term being early is indistinguishable from being wrong.

Patience and discipline are much needed when the bottom-up search for value fails to uncover any investment of merit. If you can't find something to invest in, then you are best off doing nothing at all. Warren Buffett often talks of the importance of waiting for the fat pitch.

I call investing the greatest business in the world . . . because you never have to swing. You stand at the plate, the pitcher throws you General Motors at 47! U.S. Steel at 39! and nobody calls a strike on you. There's no penalty except opportunity lost. All day you wait for the pitch you like; then when the fielders are asleep, you step up and hit it.

However, most institutional investors behave like Babe Ruth at bat with 50,000 fans and the club owner yelling, "Swing, you bum!" and some guy is trying to pitch him an intentional walk. They know if they don't take a swing at the next pitch, the guy will say, "Turn in your uniform."

In further developing this analogy, Buffett often refers to *The Science of Hitting*, a book written by Red Sox legend Ted Williams. In his book, Williams describes part of the secret to his phenomenal .344 career batting average. The theory behind Williams's extraordinary success was really quite simple (as many of the best ideas generally are). He split the strike zone into 77 cells, each of which made up the size of a baseball, and rather than swing at anything that made its way into the strike zone, he would swing only at balls within his best cells—the sweet spot—the ones he knew he could hit. If balls didn't enter one of his best cells, he simply waited for the next one—even if it meant striking out now and then.

Just as Williams wouldn't swing at everything, investors should wait for the fat pitch. Thus when the bottom-up search for opportunities fails, investors would be well advised to hold cash. As the Sage of Omaha has said

"Holding cash is uncomfortable, but not as uncomfortable as doing something stupid."

Seth Klarman picks up on the baseball metaphor in his brilliant book, *Margin of Safety*, and writes "Most institutional investors feel compelled to be fully invested at all times. They act as if an umpire were calling balls and strikes—mostly strikes—thereby forcing them to swing at almost every pitch and forego batting selectivity for frequency." As such, he urges money managers to act almost like a couch potato; ultimately you only want to put things to work when you see very good opportunities, and you should have the patience to sit on it. As Klarman puts it:

In a world in which most investors appear interested in figuring out how to make money every second and chase the idea du jour, there's also something validating about the message that it's okay to do nothing and wait for opportunities to present themselves or to pay off. That's lonely and contrary a lot of the time, but reminding yourself that that's what it takes is quite helpful.

Part of the problem for investors is that they expect investing to be exciting—largely thanks to the bubblevision. However, as Paul Samuelson once opined, "Investing should be dull. It shouldn't be exciting. Investing should be more like watching paint dry or watching grass grow. If you want excitement, take $800 and go to Las Vegas, although it is not easy to get rich in Las Vegas, at Churchill Downs, or at the local Merrill Lynch office."

The legendary Bob Kirby once wrote of the "Coffee Can Portfolio"—in which investors would have to put stocks and then not touch them—an idea he described as being passively active. As Kirby noted,

> I suspect the notion is not likely to be popular among investment managers, because, if widely adopted, it might radically change the structure of our industry and might substantially diminish the number of souls able to sustain opulent life-styles through the money management profession.
>
> The Coffee Can Portfolio concept harkens back to the Old West, when people put their valuable possessions in a coffee can and kept it under the mattress. That coffee can involved no transaction costs, administrative costs, or any other costs. The success of the program depended entirely on the wisdom and foresight used to select the objects to be placed in the coffee can to begin with.
>
> What kind of results would good money managers produce without all that activity? The answer lies in another question. Are we traders, or are we

really investors? Most good money managers are probably investors deep down inside. But quotrons and news services, and computers that churn out daily investment results make them act like traders. They start with sound research that identifies attractive companies in promising industries on a longer-term horizon. Then, they trade those stocks two or three times a year based on month-to-month news developments and rumors of all shapes and sizes.*

Perhaps Blaise Pascal put it best when he said "All men's miseries derive from not being able to sit in a quiet room alone." Alternatively, as Winnie-the-Pooh pointed out, "Never underestimate the value of doing nothing."

*Robert Kirby, "The Coffee Can Portfolio," *Journal of Portfolio Management* 29 (1984): 101–112.

Chapter Fourteen

Inside the Mind of a Lemming

~

Becoming a Contrarian Investor

As Warren Buffett observed, "A pack of lemmings looks like a group of rugged individualists compared with Wall Street when it gets a concept in its teeth." Of course, this is a highly defamatory statement with respect to lemmings.

A willingness to subjugate one's own thoughts for those of a group is a sadly common behavioral affliction. Take a look at the four lines in Exhibit 14.1. Your task is

EXHIBIT 14.1   Pick the Line

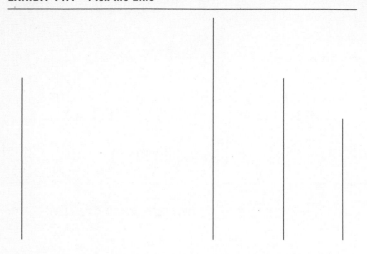

to pick which of the lines on the right most closely matches the line on the left.

If you are like most people this won't be a huge challenge. One of the lines is clearly too short, one is obviously too long, and one fits the Goldilocks outcome of just about right.

But what if you were in a room with seven other people, each of whom declared that the longest line was the closest match? Would you stick to your guns or would you bend in the face of a clear unanimous majority?

Of course, a rugged individual like you, would stick to their guns, right? Well, the evidence casts serious doubt on people's ability to maintain their independence in the face of pressure.

Experiments like the one on page 168 have been relatively commonplace since the 1950s.* The basic setup is that you are one person in a group of eight or so. Unknown to you, the other participants all work for the experimenter. The room is set up so that each subject gives his or her answer in turn, with the one true subject always going last. Under these conditions, psychologists have found that people conformed to the incorrect majority view approximately a third of the time. Three-quarters of the subjects conformed on at least one round, and one-third of the subjects conformed on more than half of the rounds.

Interestingly, experiments have found that varying the group size has virtually no impact on the likelihood of someone conforming. As soon as there were at least three people giving an incorrect answer, then about one third of subjects started to conform to the group judgment.

Recent evidence from neuroscientists further increases our understanding of what is actually happening when people conform.† Rather than using the straightline test,

---

*S. Asch, "Effects of Group Pressure upon the Modification and Distortion of Judgement," in *Groups, Leadership and Men,* ed. H. Guetzkow (New York: Carnegie Press, 1951).

†G.S. Berns, J. Chappelow , C.F. Zink, G. Pagnoni, M.E. Martin-Skurski, and J. Richards, "Neurobiological Correlates of Social Conformity and Independence During Mental Rotation," *Biological Psychiatry* 58 (2005): 245–253.

the researchers used a 3-D image rotation task, in which two images are shown and the people have to decide if the second image is a rotation of the first.

While harder than the simple straightline test, when people performed this test alone they did remarkably well, getting nearly 90 percent of the answers right. Unfortunately, a very different performance was witnessed when they could see the answers given by other members of the group. The rate of correct answers dropped to 59 percent—statistically no better than if they had flipped a coin to make the decision.

Being neuroscientists, this game was being played while the subjects were undergoing a brain scan (an MRI). The researchers found that when people went with the group answer they seemed to show a decrease in activity of the parts of the brain associated with logical thinking—the C-system. Simply put, they seemed to stop thinking.

The Pain of Going against the Crowd

Not only did participants stop thinking, but when a subject conflicted with the group a very specific part of the brain lit up—our old friend the amygdala, the brain's center of emotional processing and fear. In effect, nonconformity triggered fear in people. Going against the crowd makes people scared.

Not only does going against the herd trigger fear, but it can cause pain as well.* In this experiment, participants were told to play a computer game while having their brains scanned. Players thought they were playing in a three-way game with two other people, throwing a ball back and forth. In fact, the two other players were computer controlled. After a period of three-way play, the two other "players" began to exclude the participant by throwing the ball back and forth between themselves. This social exclusion generated brain activity in the anterior cingulated cortex and the insula, both of which are also activated by real physical pain.

Doing something different from the crowd is the investment equivalent of seeking out social pain. As a contrarian investor, you buy the stocks that everyone else is selling, and sell the stocks that everyone else is buying. This is social pain. The psychological results suggest that following such a strategy is really like having your arm broken on a regular basis—not fun!

Fortunately, although painful, a strategy of being contrarian is integral to successful investment. As Sir John Templeton put it, "It is impossible to produce superior performance unless you do something different from

---

*N. Eisenberger, M. Lieberman, and K. Williams, "Does Rejection Hurt? An fMRI Study of Social Exclusion," *Science* 302:5643 (2003): 290–292.

the majority," or as Keynes pointed out "The central principle of investment is to go contrary to the general opinion on the grounds that if everyone agreed about its merits, the investment is inevitably too dear and therefore unattractive."

Research shows that Templeton and Keynes were spot on.* The stocks institutional fund managers are busy buying are outperformed by the stocks they are busy selling. For instance, if stocks are assigned to different port-folios, based upon the persistence of institutional net trade (that is, the number of consecutive quarters for which institutions are net buyers or net sellers is recorded), and then the performance of the portfolios is tracked over a two-year time horizon, there is a 17 percent return difference—the stock that the institutions sold the most outperformed the market by around 11 percent, and the stocks they purchased the most underperformed by 6 percent.

The Carrot of Conformity

Obviously the avoidance of pain stands out as a key factor in determining whether people choose to conform or not. However, if pain is the stick, then praise is the carrot. Given that so many professional investors make decisions

---

*A. Dasgupta, A. Prat, and M. Verado, "The Price of Conformism" (Unpublished paper).

in groups, this dynamic is an important one to understand. Psychologists have studied groups and asked them to rate members in terms of competency. It shouldn't come as a great surprise (given all you now know about mental pitfalls such as confirmatory bias) that members of groups rate themselves higher, and are rated higher by other members of the group, when they bring information that is common or shared to the group. Those bringing divergent perspectives were effectively shunned.

Indeed, groups show a disturbing habit of focusing upon common information. Researchers set up a clever experiment that demonstrates the essence of this problem.* Participants were trying to choose between three candidates running for president of the student council. The information made available was designed so that candidate A was the best candidate.

When reviewing the profiles and using all the information on the various candidates, 67 percent of the subjects individually selected candidate A. To see how the groups performed, the experiment was run twice more. On the first run, all the participants had all the information available to them—just as they did when making the

---

*G. Stasser and W. Titus, "Pooling of Unshared Information in Group Decision Making: Solving a Problem versus Making a Judgment," *Journal of Personality and Social Psychology* 48 (1985): 1467–1478.

selection alone. The groups actually performed better, with 83 percent selecting candidate A.

However, on the next run, some of the information was made available to all the participants, but some was distributed among the group so only one of the group knew about it. In fact, the relevant information on candidate A was widely disbursed among the group. When faced with this situation, the groups seemed to spend nearly all their time talking about the information they shared in common, rather than trying to uncover and aggregate the scattered information. Only 18 percent selected candidate A.

The Dangers of Groupthink

Groups have powerful self-reinforcing mechanisms at work. These can lead to group polarization—a tendency for members of the group to end up in a more extreme position than they started in because they have heard the views repeated frequently.

At the extreme limit of group behavior is groupthink. This occurs when a group makes faulty decisions because group pressures lead to a deterioration of "mental efficiency, reality testing, and moral judgment."* The original work was conducted with reference to the Vietnam War and

*I. Janis, *Groupthink*. (New York: Houghton Mifflin, 1972).

the Bay of Pigs fiasco. However, it rears its head again and again, whether it is in connection with the Challenger space shuttle disaster or the CIA intelligence failure over the WMD of Saddam Hussein.

Groupthink tends to have eight symptoms:

1. *An illusion of invulnerability.* This creates excessive optimism that encourages taking extreme risks. This is very similar to the over-optimism and over-confidence we discussed in Chapters 4 and 5.

2. *Collective rationalization.* Members of the group discount warnings and do not reconsider their assumptions. They become blind in the same ways we saw in our discussion of conservatism in Chapter 10.

3. *Belief in inherent morality.* Members believe in the rightness of their cause and therefore ignore the ethical or moral consequences of their decisions.

4. *Stereotyped views of out-groups.* Negative views of "enemy" make effective responses to conflict seem unnecessary. Remember how those who wouldn't go along with the dot-com bubble were dismissed as simply not getting it.

5. *Direct pressure on dissenters.* Members are under pressure not to express arguments against any of the group's views.

6. *Self-censorship*. Doubts and deviations from the perceived group consensus are not expressed.

7. *Illusion of unanimity*. The majority view and judgments are assumed to be unanimous.

8. *"Mind guards" are appointed*. Members protect the group and the leader from information that is problematic or contradictory to the group's cohesiveness, view, and/or decisions. This is confirmatory bias writ large.

No less a sage than the mighty Robert Shiller has described his struggles with conformity and groupthink. In an article for the *New York Times* written in late 2008, he says, "While I warned about the bubbles I believed were developing in the stock and housing markets, I did so very gently, and felt vulnerable expressing such quirky views. Deviating too far from consensus leaves one feeling potentially ostracized from the group, with the risk that one may be terminated."

Echoing Shiller's perspective, I have often pondered the possibility that academic finance is a prime example of groupthink at work. The obsession with the neat elegance of mathematical models and the love of the efficient markets hypothesis that dominates economics and finance departments strike me as the result of a classic example of groupthink. Those who challenge the orthodoxy are shunned, and young professors hoping for tenure are discouraged from expressing doubts and concerns. The journals and their editors act as mind guards for the community, suppressing views that might contradict the conventional wisdom.

Alone in a Crowd of Sheep

One final word of warning to all budding contrarians—we all like to think we are independent thinkers. Sadly, it is just another one of our failures to actually see our behavior as it really is (known as the introspection bias we discussed in the Introduction). We see others' behavior as a demonstration of their underlying nature, while we see our own actions as driven by the circumstances we face (the fundamental attribution error).

Both of these biases come together to convince us that we are independent thinkers. However, psychologists have explored the foundations of this belief that each of us thinks we act without influence from the crowd, while we see others as being highly influenced by peer behavior.*

They asked 40 owners of iPods how influenced they were by the trendiness of the product relative to their peers. The scale went from one (much less than average) to nine (much more than average), with five as average. So the neutral answer was clearly five. However, the average

---

*E. Pronin, J. Berger, and S. Molouki, "Alone in a Crowd of Sheep: Asymmetric Perceptions of Conformity and Their Roots in an Introspection Illusion," *Journal of Personality and Social Psychology* 92 (2007): 585–595.

response from the participants was a score of only 3.3, which indicates they thought they were all much less influenced by the trendiness of the iPod than the average.

In another experiment, participants were asked to "Imagine that [you are/Carol is] shopping at a clothing store, and [you are/Carol is] deciding what pair of jeans to buy." They were then asked to indicate what it might mean to conform in this situation by choosing from two options. One option was focused on internal information: "While [you are/Carol is] looking at different jeans [you think/she thinks] about whether [your/ her] friends have been wearing them." Alternatively, the other opinion emphasized observable behavior: "[You/Carol] ends up buying a pair of jeans that many of [your/her] friends have been wearing lately."

Multiple scenarios were presented in this fashion. The findings show that when the situations were phrased in terms of others (i.e., Carol), then the options involving observable behavior were selected much more often than those based on internal information (65 versus 35 percent). However, when the situations were expressed in the first person, then the internal information option (less consistent with conformity) was selected far more often (65 versus 35).

It isn't easy being a contrarian. Make no mistake about it, even the very best investors have to overcome the demon of conformity. Overcoming this particular demon effectively requires three elements. The first is highlighted by the legendary hedge fund manager Michael Steinhardt, who urged investors to have the courage to be different. He said, "The hardest thing over the years has been having the courage to go against the dominant wisdom of the time, to have a view that is at variance with the present consensus and bet that view."

The second element is to be a critical thinker. As Joel Greenblatt has opined, "You can't be a good value investor without being an independent thinker—you're seeing valuations that the market is not appreciating. But it's critical that you understand why the market isn't seeing the value."

Finally, you must have the perseverance and grit to stick to your principles. As Ben Graham noted, "If you believe that the value approach is inherently sound then devote yourself to that principle. Stick to it, and don't be led astray by Wall Street's fashions, illusions and its constant chase after the fast dollar. Let me emphasize that it does not take genius to be a successful value analyst, what it needs is, first, reasonably good intelligence; second, sound principles of operation; and third, and most important, firmness of character."

Only by mastering all three of these elements will you be able to stand against the herd and reap the investment returns.

Chapter Fifteen

You Gotta Know When to Fold Them

~

When it's Time to Sell an Investment

TIME FOR ANOTHER GAME—IF YOU DARE.

This time, let's toss a fair coin. If you loose you must pay me $100.

What is the minimum amount that you would need to win to make that bet attractive?

Let's assume you can only deal in one dollar units. The rational response is therefore an answer above $100. In fact, if you are risk neutral you should be willing to play for $100. However, when I ask this question I generally get a much, much higher response than $100. In fact, the average response from the 600 fund managers who have taken my test is just over $200. That is, they need to win twice the amount they may lose before they will consider this a good bet.

This result is typical for such a question. In general people hate losses somewhere between two and two-and-a-half times as much as they enjoy equivalent gains. This is a property known as loss aversion.

In my sample of fund managers we got the full range of responses from those who required $1000 or more (over ten times as much as they stood to lose) to those who would have accepted just $50. I guess the former thought I was pathologically incapable of using a fair coin, the latter simply loved giving money away.

In general, people's performance on the cognitive reflection task (CRT) from the introduction of this book is reasonably correlated with the degree of loss aversion they display. For instance, those who got only one of the CRT questions correct wanted an average of $300 to accept the bet. Those who got two questions right wanted $250, and those who managed to get all three CRT questions correct wanted $165. The more CRT questions you got right, the less likely you suffer extreme loss aversion.

Loss aversion shows up in all sorts of areas, including professional golf.* In a recent study, researchers examined some 1.6 million putts in PGA tournaments. The aim in each tournament is, obviously, for each golfer to minimize the total number of shots required to get around 72 holes. Thus golfers should only care about their overall tournament score.

However, the researchers found that golfers were subject to loss aversion. When golfers were shooting a birdie putt (that would earn them a score one stroke under par) or shooting an eagle putt (that would earn them a score two strokes under par), they were significantly less accurate than when they attempted otherwise similar putts for par or over par. On average, golfers make their birdie putts two to three percentage points less often than they make comparable par putts. For instance, when looking at all putts less than 24 inches from the hole, professional golfers make some 86 percent of the putts for par. But when the putts are for a birdie, only 82 percent of the putts are successful. This finding is consistent with loss aversion; players invest more focus when putting for par to avoid suffering a loss.

*D. Pope and M. Schweitzer, "Is Tiger Woods Loss Averse?" (Unpublished paper, 2009).

Indeed, in an interview Tiger Woods said, "Any time you make big par putts, I think it's more important to make those than birdie putts. You don't ever want to drop a shot. The psychological difference between dropping a shot and making a birdie, I just think it's bigger to make a par putt."

This bias doesn't come cheap. In professional golf, improving a score by one stroke pays handsomely. On average, the top 20 golfers earned nearly $4 million in tournament earnings in 2008. If each player had improved their score by one stroke in each of the tournaments in which they participated (assuming that other players' scores remained unchanged), the golfers would have earned an additional $1.1 million on average (a 22 percent increase in their winnings).

We Are Not Alone (or Perhaps Not Even That Evolved!)

Researchers have even explored loss aversion in capuchin monkeys.* Capuchin monkeys split off from our evolutionary tree somewhere around 35 million years ago, so they are a pretty distant relative compared to, say, the chimpanzees, who separated from us a mere six million or so years ago.

*K. Chen, V. Lakshminarayanan, and L. Santos, "How Basic are Behavioral Biases? Evidence from Capuchin-Monkey Trading Behavior," *Journal of Political Economy* 114 (2006): 517–537.

You may well be asking how on earth you test to see if capuchin monkeys are loss averse. The answer is to play games with them. In fact, you play two games with them. In the first game, the capuchins were given one grape and, dependent on a coin flip, either retained the original grape or won a bonus grape. In the second game, the capuchin started out owning the bonus grape and, once again dependent on a coin flip, either kept the two grapes or lost one. These two games are in fact the same gamble, with identical odds, but one is framed as a potential win and the other as a potential loss.

How did the capuchins react? They far preferred to take a gamble on the potential gain than the potential loss. Just in case you are wondering how you can tell which game capuchin monkeys preferred, two experimenters play the games, and the monkeys returned predominately to just one of the experimenters—effectively showing their preference. Such behavior is not what an economics textbook would predict. The laws of economics state that these two gambles, because they represent such small stakes, should be treated equally. The monkeys were clearly displaying loss aversion, just as we do.

Myopia and Loss Aversion

As if it wasn't bad enough that loss aversion may well be ingrained into our genetic code, we make it worse on ourselves by being myopic (which is an overt focus on the short term). The more you check your portfolio the more likely you are to encounter a loss simply because of the volatile nature of stock prices. If only we could avoid the temptation to keep checking our portfolios! Researchers have found that people are willing to invest more when they see the performance of their holdings infrequently.*

Imagine you are taking part in a lottery. You are assigned one of three colors—red, white, or blue. Whether you win or not depends on someone picking your color from a hat that contains all three colors in equal number. The odds on your winning are obviously 33 percent. In each round you will be given $100, and you must decide how much of this $100 you would like to wager. If you win you will make two-and-a-half times the amount you wager. If you lose, you lose the wager you placed.

Two versions of this particular game were played. Each consisted of nine rounds. In the first version, players announced how much they would be prepared to wager round by round. In the second version they announced how much they would wager each round, but rounds were grouped into threes.

*M.S. Haigh and J.A. List, "Do Professional Traders Exhibit Myopic Loss Aversion? An Experimental Analysis," *Journal of Finance* LX (2005): 523–534.

Both students and professional traders have played this game. When asked round by round, the students wagered an average of $51, but when asked to wager over groups of three rounds they were prepared to bet $62. The traders wagered only $45 when asked round by round, but wanted to bet $75 per round when rounds were grouped into three games. The traders displayed more myopic loss aversion than the students. So much for the idea that experience and incentives will wipe out behavioral biases.

In his wonderful *The Little Book that Beats the Market*, Joel Greenblatt points out that loss aversion is one of the many behavioral biases that prevent us from investing along the lines of his magic formula. He writes, "Imagine diligently watching those stocks each day as they do worse than the market average over the course of many months or even years. . . . The magic formula port-folio fared poorly relative to the market average in five out of every 12 months tested. For full year periods the magic formula portfolio failed to beat the market average once every four years." A lot of us value managers know exactly how this feels.

It never ceases to amaze me that some fund managers actually have access to their portfolio's performance in real time; they can see exactly how much they are winning or losing second by second. I can't imagine many more destructive practices that this. If I've done my homework, and selected stocks that I think represent good value over the long term, why on earth would I want to sit and watch their performance day by day, let alone second by second. I rarely examine the performance of my personal port-folio, as it is full of positions that should perform well in the long term but certainly aren't guaranteed to do so without short-term losses.

This perspective is shared by Seth Klarman. He stated that if the technology existed to permit real-time performance measurement of his portfolios, he wouldn't want it, since it would run completely contrary to his long-term focus. Yet, investment managers can usually be found scurrying around to achieve superior daily or weekly perfor-mance, even though their proper goal ought to be to realize substantial gains farther down the road. This type of behavior makes little sense and can really dent your returns over the long term.

Why You Can't Bring Yourself to Sell

We have already seen what happens when investors suf-fer a loss—they go into a terminal shut down (Chapter 2). However, there are subtle but important differences between behavior after loss and behavior that involves the risk of incurring a loss.

Consider the following concurrent choices:

A. A sure gain of $24,000

Or

B. A 25 percent chance of $100,000 and a 75 percent chance of gaining nothing

And

C. A sure loss of $75,000

Or

D. A 75 percent chance of losing $100,000 and a 25 percent chance of losing nothing

Experiment after experiment has revealed that most people choose A and D; however, that combination doesn't make a lot of sense. The expected gain of option B is $25,000, so choosing A over B is consistent with risk aversion. However, the choice of D over C is risk seeking. The expected value of option D is –$75,000, but C offers that loss for sure, whereas D has a chance of losing you $100,000.

Putting the dislike of losses and the willingness to gamble in the face of potential losses together gives us some powerful insights into investors' behavior. For some reason, in some bizarre mental world, people believe that a loss isn't a loss until they realize it. This belief tends to lead to investors holding onto their losing stocks and selling their winning stocks—known as the disposition effect.

Terry Odean (whom you met in Chapter 4) has explored this bad habit among individual investors.* He has examined data from a discount brokerage for about 10,000 accounts from 1987 to 1993. The purchases and sales for each account had been recorded. Odean found that investors held losing stocks for a median of 124 days and held winning stocks for a median of 102 days. He also calculated the percentage of losing positions that were realized (as a percentage of all losing stocks held) and the percentage of winning positions that were realized (as a percentage of all winning stocks held).

Lo and behold, Odean discovered that these individual investors sold an average of 15 percent of all winning positions and only 9 percent of all losing positions. That is to say, individual investors are 1.7 times as likely to sell a winning stock than a losing stock.

---

*Terrance Odean, "Are Investors Reluctant to Realize Their Losses?" *Journal of Finance* LIII (1998): 1775–1798.

One of the most common reasons for holding onto a stock is the belief that it will bounce back subsequently. This could be motivated by any number of potential psychological flaws ranging from over-optimism (Chapter 3) and overconfidence (Chapter 4) to self-attribution bias (Chapter 12). Odean decided to investigate whether investors were correctly betting on recovery in the losers they continued to hold. Sadly, he found that the winners that were sold outperformed the losers that continued to be held by an average of 3.4 percent per annum.

As mentioned before, professional investors are often very dismissive of such findings. In general, they assume that all of this behavioral finance theorizing applies to individual investors but not to them (talk about overconfident!).

Such overconfidence seems to be sadly misplaced. Andrea Frazzini has investigated the behavior of mutual fund managers, and has discovered that even such seasoned professionals seem to suffer loss aversion.* Frazzini analyzed the holdings and transactions of mutual funds between 1980 and 2002. He ended up with a sample of nearly 30,000 U.S. domestic mutual funds.

Across all funds, he found that 17.6 percent of all gains were realized, but only 14.5 percent of all losses were realized.

---

*Andrea Frazzini, "The Disposition Effect and Under-Reaction to News," *Journal of Finance* LXI (2006) 2017–2046.

So professional investors were 1.2 times as likely to sell a winning stock rather than a losing stock. However, Frazzini took his analysis one step further. He ranked the mutual funds by the performance achieved over the last 12 months. The best-performing funds were those with the highest percentage of losses realized (i.e., the least loss averse). The best-performing funds are less than 1.2 times more likely to sell a winning position than a losing position. The worst-performing funds had the lowest percentage of realized losses. In fact, the worst performing funds showed about the same degree of loss aversion as the individual investors. They were 1.7 times more likely to sell a winning position than a losing position. So, professional investors are just as likely to suffer from the disposition effect as the rest of us.

Stop losses may be a useful form of pre-commitment that help alleviate the disposition effect in markets that witness momentum. Indeed the disposition effect can generate the underreaction that characterises momentum. Suppose a stock has a good earnings report, and the price rises. The market will witness selling as investors seem to have little trouble in selling winners; thus the price doesn't reach its full level in one go. Conversely, if a company witnesses a bad earnings report, it share price might fall, but investors are unwilling to realize their losses. They hold onto the stock hoping it will recover. So prices adjust to new information only slowly in a world where investors display the disposition effect. Stop losses can act as triggers to prevent you sliding down the slippery slope of the disposition effect.

The Endowment Effect

Imagine you had bought a bottle of wine for $15 a few years ago. The wine has now appreciated vastly in price so that at auction a bottle would now fetch something north of $150. Would you be prepared to buy a bottle or sell your existing stock? The most frequently encountered answer is a resounding "no" to both questions. When faced with this situation, people are generally unwilling to either buy or sell the wine.

Let's try another case. Imagine you own a stock that has lost 30 percent of its value in the last three months. Given what we know about loss aversion, the chances are you will stick with it. However, imagine you go and make a cup of tea, and while you are standing over the kettle your four year old nephew starts randomly pressing buttons on your PC looking for his favorite Thomas the Tank Engine game. You come back to your desk to find your nephew has somehow inadvertently sold your entire position. What do you do? Will you buy the shares you were previously so reluctant to sell? When asked this question almost no one wants to buy back the stock.

These two scenarios provide us with examples of inaction inertia also known as *the status quo bias*. It is also an example of the *endowment effect*. Simply put, the endowment effect says that once you own something you start to place a higher value on it than others would.

The endowment effect is relatively easy to demonstrate in a classroom. You randomly give half a class of students a mug (or a pen, or anything else). Then tell the class that a market will be formed in which students with mugs can sell them to students without mugs who might want them. Presumably, since the mugs were randomly distributed, roughly half the people should wish to trade. So the predicted volume level is 50 percent. However, volumes in such markets are usually a fraction of the amount that might be expected. Indeed, in many experiments the actual volume level is closer to 10 percent. The key reason for the lack of transactions is a massive gap in prices between the would-be buyers and sellers.

Mugs such as the one used in this experiment retailed for $6 at the university store. Those who had mugs were willing to sell them from $5.25 on average. Those who didn't have mugs weren't willing to spend more than $2.50 to acquire one. So, despite being given the mugs only minutes before, the act of ownership led sellers to ask for double the amount that buyers were willing to actually pay for the mug. Ownership seems to massively distort people's perceptions of value.

Does this endowment effect stem from a reluctance to buy (cheapskates) or a reluctance to sell (asking too much)? The relative importance of these two factors can be assessed by introducing a third category of player into the market. Rather than having just buyers and sellers, experimenters have introduced *choosers*. As before, mugs are distributed across the class randomly. The sellers were asked if they would be willing to sell their mugs at prices ranging from $0.25 to $9.25. A second group, the buyers, were asked if they would be willing to buy a mug over the same range of prices. A third group, the choosers, were not given a mug but were asked to choose, for each of the prices, whether they would rather receive a mug or the equivalent amount of money.

In theory, the choosers and the sellers are in exactly the same situation—both groups are deciding at each price between the mug and the amount of money. The only difference between the two groups is that the choosers don't have physical possession of a mug. However, as Yoga Berra pointed out, "In theory, there is no difference between theory and practice. In practice, there is!"

Choosers' prices are generally higher (on average around 50 percent higher) than the buyers' prices, but are still well below the prices set by the sellers. Sellers had prices that were on average nearly three times greater than the buyers were willing to pay, and nearly double the amount the choosers would have been willing to trade at. This represents clear evidence of the endowment effect being driven by a reluctance of owners to part with their asset, even though they may have only actually owned the item in question for a matter of minutes.

Think about these effects the next time you're considering a particular company. If you already hold stock in that company, you may actually impute a higher value than is warranted, simply because you already own the shares. Lee Ainslie of Maverick Capital is aware of this kind of problem. He tests his conviction by gauging whether the name is a buy or a sell; there is no hold. Ainslie says, "Either this security deserves incremental capital at the current price point or it doesn't—in which case, let's sell it and put the money to work in a security that deserves that incremental capital."

Figuring out how to act in the face of losses is one of the biggest challenges any investor can face. As fund manager Richard Pzena puts it, "I believe the biggest way you add value as a value investor is how you behave on those down-25 percent situations. Sometimes you should buy more, sometimes you should get out, and sometimes you should stay put. . . . We probably hold tight 40 percent of the time, and split 50/50 between buying more and getting out."

Christopher Browne of Tweedy Browne makes a further useful distinction when it comes to selling an investment. He points out that we should:

Make a clear distinction when selling between "compounders" and cigar butt stocks. Once the cigar butts come back, you know to get out because they're just going to go down again. With something like Johnson & Johnson, though, you make a judgment call when it hits intrinsic value, based on your confidence in its ability to compound returns and what your alternatives are.

This dichotomy between "cigar butts" and "compounders" is an important one for investors to understand. Warren Buffett has described Ben Graham's (his mentor) investment style as cigar-butt investing—that is, buying really cheap stocks almost regardless of the underlying industry economics, and then selling them when they get close to intrinsic value. Stocks that Browne describes as compounders will tend to grow their intrinsic value over time, allowing the investor to reap the rewards over a longer time period (assuming that market price doesn't get far ahead of intrinsic value).

I am not a big country and western fan (frankly I prefer hard rock), but my dad was a big Kenny Rogers fan, and the words to his song, "The Gambler," could well serve as a useful reminder to investors: "You gotta know when to hold them, know when to fold them, know when to walk away, and know when to run. You never count your money while you're sitting at the table, there be time enough for counting when the dealings done."

Chapter Sixteen

Process, Process, Process

That One Thing You Can Control

Watching the Olympics and listening to several of the successful athletes, one of the inane questions from the interviewers often seemed to be, "What was going through your mind before the event? Were you thinking of the gold?" Time and time again the competitors responded that they were focused on the process, not the outcome. Along similar lines I came across the following post by Paul DePodesta on his blog, "It Might Be

Dangerous . . . You Go First" from June 10, 2008. (If you want to read it go to http://itmightbedangerous.blogspot .com.) For those who don't know DePodesta, he is a baseball front-office assistant for the San Diego Padres and was formerly the general manager of the Los Angeles Dodgers. For those who have read Michael Lewis's *Moneyball*, DePodesta will need no introduction.

Many years ago I was playing blackjack in Las Vegas on a Saturday night in a packed casino. I was sitting at third base, and the player who was at first base was playing horribly. He was definitely taking advantage of the free drinks, and it seemed as though every twenty minutes he was dipping into his pocket for more cash. On one particular hand the player was dealt 17 with his first two cards. The dealer was set to deal the next set of cards and passed right over the player until he stopped her, saying: "Dealer, I want a hit!" She paused, almost feeling sorry for him, and said, "Sir, are you sure?" He said yes, and the dealer dealt the card. Sure enough, it was a four.

The place went crazy, high fives all around, everybody hootin' and hollerin', and you know what the dealer said? The dealer looked at the player, and with total sincerity, said: "Nice hit." I thought,

"Nice hit? Maybe it was a nice hit for the casino, but it was a terrible hit for the player! The decision isn't justified just because it worked."

Well, I spent the rest of that weekend wandering around the casino, largely because I had lost all of my money playing blackjack, thinking about all of these different games and how they work. The fact of the matter is that all casino games have a winning process—the odds are stacked in the favor of the house. That doesn't mean they win every single hand or every roll of the dice, but they do win more often than not. Don't misunderstand me—the casino is absolutely concerned about outcomes.

However, their approach to securing a good outcome is a laser-like focus on process . . . right down to the ruthless pit boss. We can view baseball through the same lens. Baseball is certainly an outcome driven business, as we get charged with a W or an L 162 times a year (or 163 times every once in a while). Furthermore, we know we cannot possibly win every single time. In fact, winning just 60% of the time is a great season, a percentage that far exceeds house odds in most games. Like a casino, it appears as though baseball is all about outcomes, but just think about all of the processes that are in play during the course of just one game or even just one at-bat.

In having this discussion years ago with Michael
Mauboussin, who wrote *More Than You Know* (a great
book), he showed me a very simple matrix by Russo
and Schoemaker in *Winning Decisions* that explains
this concept:

	Good Outcome	Bad Outcome
Good Process	Deserved success	Bad break
Bad Process	Dumb luck	Poetic justice

We all want to be in the upper left box—deserved
success resulting from a good process. This is generally where the casino lives. I'd like to think that
this is where the Oakland A's and San Diego Padres
have been during the regular seasons. The box in
the upper right, however, is the tough reality we all
face in industries that are dominated by uncertainty.
A good process can lead to a bad outcome in the
real world. In fact, it happens all the time. This is
what happened to the casino when a player hit on 17
and won. I'd like to think this is what happened to
the A's and Padres during the post-seasons.

As tough as a good process/bad outcome combination is, nothing compares to the bottom left: bad
process/good outcome. This is the wolf in sheep's
clothing that allows for one-time success but almost

always cripples any chance of sustained success—the player hitting on 17 and getting a four. Here's the rub: it's incredibly difficult to look in the mirror after a victory, any victory, and admit that you were lucky. If you fail to make that admission, however, the bad process will continue and the good outcome that occurred once will elude you in the future. Quite frankly, this is one of the things that makes Billy Beane [General Manager of the Oakland A's] as good as he is. He is quick to notice good luck embedded in a good outcome, and he refuses to pat himself on the back for it.

At the Padres, we want to win every game we play at every level and we want to be right on every single player decision we make. We know it's not going to happen, because there is too much uncertainty . . . too much we cannot control. That said, we can control the process.

Championship teams will occasionally have a bad process and a good outcome.

Championship organizations, however, reside exclusively in the upper half of the matrix.

To me the similarities between DePodesta's points on process in baseball and process in investment are blindingly obvious. We obsess with outcomes over which we have no direct control. However, we can and do control the process by which we invest. As investors, this is what we should focus upon. The management of return is impossible, the management of risk is illusory, but *process* is the one thing we can exert an influence over.

Ben Graham knew the importance of focusing upon process. He wrote:

> I recall to those of you who are bridge players the emphasis that bridge experts place on playing a hand right rather than on playing it successfully. Because, as you know, if you play it right you are going to make money and if you play it wrong you lose money—in the long run. There is a beautiful little story about the man who was the weaker bridge player of the husband-and-wife team. It seems he bid a grand slam, and at the end he said very triumphantly to his wife "I saw you making faces at me all the time, but you notice I not only bid this grand slam but I made it. What can you say about that?" And his wife replied very dourly, "If you had played it right you would have lost it."

The Psychology of Process

The need to focus on process rather than outcomes is critical in investing. As we have seen in this Little Book, there are no magic short cuts to being a good investor. The investors I have mentioned in the various chapters have come across behavioral biases in themselves, and have tried to find a way to overcome these innate tendencies.

In investing, outcomes are highly unstable because they involve an integral of time. Effectively, it is perfectly possible to be "right" over a five-year view and "wrong" on a six-month view, and vice versa. We also have to deal with the fact that price volatility is several orders of magnitude greater than fundamental volatility.

People often judge a past decision by its ultimate outcome rather than basing it on the quality of the decision at the time it was made, given what was known at that time. This is outcome bias.

Imagine you are asked to rate the soundness of the physician's decision process (not outcome) in the following case.

A 55-year old man had a heart condition. He had to stop working because of chest pain. He enjoyed his work and did not want to stop. His pain also interfered with other things, such as travel and recreation. A type of bypass operation would relieve his pain and increase his life expectancy from age 65 to age 70. However, 8 percent of the people who have this operation die from the operation itself. His physician decided to go ahead with the operation. The operation succeeded.

Evaluate the physician's decision to go ahead with the operation, on the following scale:

3—Clearly correct, and the opposite decision would be inexcusable

2—Correct, all things considered

1—Correct, but the opposite would be reasonable too

0—The decision and its opposite are equally good

–1—Incorrect, but not unreasonable

–2—Incorrect, all things considered

–3—Incorrect and inexcusable

Now imagine the same task except that in this alternative setting, the operation was unsuccessful and the patient died. Of course, the correctness of the physician's decision should not be a function of the outcome, since clearly the doctor couldn't have known the outcome before the event. However, when people are given scenarios such as these the decision is always rated as much better if the outcome is good.*

Psychological evidence also shows that focusing on outcomes can create all sorts of unwanted actions. For instance, in a world in which short-term performance is

*J. Baron and J.C. Hershey, "Outcome Bias in Decision Evaluation," *Journal of Personality and Social Psychology* 54 (1988): 569–579.

everything, fund managers may end up buying stocks they find easy to justify to their clients, rather than those that represent the best opportunity.

In general, holding people accountable for outcomes tends to increase the following:*

- Focus on outcomes with a higher certainty, which is known as ambiguity aversion.
- Collection and use of all information (both useful and useless).
- Preference for compromise options.
- Selection of products with average features on all measures over a product with mixed features (i.e. average on four traits, preferred to good on two and bad on two).
- Degree of loss aversion that people display.

None of these features is likely to serve investors well. Together they suggest that when every decision is measured on outcomes, investors are likely to avoid uncertainty, chase noise, and herd with the consensus. Sounds like a pretty good description of much of the investment industry to me.

*J.S. Lerner and P.E. Tetlock, "Accounting for the Effects of Accountability," *Psychological Bulletin* 125 (1999): 255–275.

Process Accountability

However, if we switch the focus from outcomes to process, things begin to change for the better. Let's imagine you work for an American brewery that was planning to distribute its nonalcoholic and light beer (as repulsive as those ideas are to me as a real ale drinker) into Europe. The data shows that both products have done about equally well in their test period.

Your task is to decide which of the two products should receive an extra $3 million in funding. The decision you make should reflect the potential benefit of the additional funding to the product and the company. You write down your decision and provide a brief explanation of the reasoning behind the decision.

Having done this, you receive the following communication from the head office. "Your recommendation to allocate the additional $3 million to the (whichever beer you chose) beer was adopted by the president of the company and implemented. As you will note on the next page, the results have been rather disappointing."

The data indicate sales and profits of the product that you had selected started okay and then went down, and finally settled in a low constant pattern of sales. The sales and profits of the alternative product were also shown. They also went up initially, then down, but ended up settling at a higher level than the product chosen by you."

You are then told that the company had decided to make an additional $10 million available in funding. However, this time the money could be split between the two beers. How would you allocate the $10 million between the two beers?

In addition you are told one of the following:

1. The information you have received is enough to make a good decision—the baseline.

Or

2. If you make particularly good or bad choices your performance would be shared with students and instructors. You are also told that your performance would be based on the outcome of the decision they took—outcome accountability.

Or

3. You are informed that your evaluation would be based on their effective use of decision strategies rather than the outcomes of those strategies. Once again, if you use particularly good or bad decision processes these would be shared with students and instructors—process accountability.

The evidence shows a marked difference in the allocations depending on which of these three statements you receive.* The group who were focused on the outcome of their decision decided to allocate an average of $5.8 million to the beer they had originally selected. This is a classic example of the sunk cost fallacy (which we saw in Chapter 9).

By comparison, the baseline subjects split the money roughly evenly, giving their previous choice $5.1 million. However, the group told to focus upon the process of decision-making rather than the outcome did much better. They only allocated $4 million to the beer that they had originally chosen, giving the majority of the money to the more popular beer.

Focusing on process seems to lead to better decisions.

The same is true in investment. Focusing upon process frees us up from the worrying about aspects of investment which we really can't control—such as return. By focusing upon process we maximize our potential to generate good long-term returns.

Unfortunately, focusing on process and its long-term benefits won't necessarily help you in the short term. During periods of underperformance, the pressure always

*I. Simonson and B. M. Straw, "Deescalation Strategies: A Comparison of Techniques for Reducing Commitment to Losing Courses of Action," *Journal of Applied Psychology* 77 (1992): 419–426.

builds to change your process. However, a sound process is capable of generating poor results, just as a bad process can generate good results. Perhaps we would all do well to remember the late great Sir John Templeton's words, "The time to reflect on your investing methods is when you are most successful, not when you are making the most mistakes," or indeed Ben Graham's exultation, "The value approach is inherently sound . . . devote yourself to that principle. Stick to it, and don't be led astray."

Conclusion

The Road to Hell Is Paved with Good Intentions

Why Promising to Be Good Just Isn't Enough

IT IS CONFESSION TIME. As anyone who knows me can attest, I am overweight (although I prefer to think of myself as simply too short for my weight). In fact, according to the body mass index which compares height to weight (designed by size fascists, I'm sure) I am on the borderline between overweight and obese.

I know how to correct this problem. I should simply eat less. However, I find this incredibly hard to actually do. So despite that fact I know how to change, I don't change, so my knowledge doesn't translate into better behavior. Rather I file the information in the category of "things I know and choose to ignore."

Brian Wansink has written a brilliant book about the psychology of food entitled *Mindless Eating*. He and his fellow researchers have found that many of the same biases I have discussed in previous chapters show up in our eating and shopping habits (evidence for the universal nature of these biases). For instance, the ease of availability influences how much we eat. When chocolates are visible and convenient, people will eat nearly three times more than when they have to walk two meters to collect one! Think about this in terms of information and the problems with information overload that we discussed in Chapter 7.

Similarly, Wansink has found evidence of anchoring effects when it comes to shopping. He presented consumers with a limit in terms of the quantity of cans of soup they were allowed to purchase. The soup was labelled as costing 79 cents (normally 89 cents) and purchasers were presented with a sign saying either "No limit per person," "Limit of four cans per person," or "Limit of twelve cans per person." When there was no limit, an average of 3.3 cans per person were purchased with total sales of 73 cans. When the four-can limit was introduced, buyers purchased an average of 3.5 cans per person, but total sales increased to 106 cans. When the 12-can limit was imposed, the average buyer purchased 7 cans and total sales soared to 188 cans. So merely suggesting a number seemed to provoke a very real reaction among consumers. As we mentioned before, this has parallels with much of the modern risk management industry.

Even the influence of groups shows up when it comes to eating. If you dine with one other person, you'll eat about 35 percent more than you would otherwise. If you eat in a group of seven or more, you'll eat nearly twice as much as you would do on your own! Talk about the power of herding.

Wansink warns of the danger of the tyranny of the moment—the point at which we find ourselves staring at the vending machine with a Mars bar beckoning to us. We know we don't need it, but we rationalize it as a chocolate hit to compensate for a stressful day. Knowledge doesn't necessarily lead to changes in behavior.

In fact, even in the most life-threatening situations, knowledge doesn't equal behavior. Researchers have examined the difference between knowledge of HIV/AIDS and its prevention, and actual sexual behavior.* In Botswana, 91 percent of men said they knew that the use of a condom could help prevent the spread of HIV/AIDS, yet only 70 percent of them used a condom. Among women the situation was even worse: 92 percent reported that they knew condoms were useful in preventing HIV/AIDS transmission, but only 63 percent used them. So even when the stakes are as high as they possibly can be (your very life depends upon it), knowledge is still not enough to alter behavior.

Simple promises to be good or to behave better are unlikely to be enough either. We all start out with good intentions. Sadly, few of us seem to end up seeing those intentions turn into a reality. For instance, people were asked to complete a questionnaire about giving blood at an upcoming donation clinic.[†] They had to rate how likely they were to give blood, and also rate on a scale of 1 (strongly disagree) to 9 (strongly agree) a series of statements concerning their attitudes on the subject, including a final question which read, "Right now, as I think about it, I strongly intend to donate blood at the July 14–22 blood donation clinic." This was used to gauge participants' current intention strength.

*T. Dinkleman, J.A. Levinsohn, and R. Majelantle, "When Knowledge Isn't Enough: HIV/AIDS Information and Risk Behavior in Botswana" (NBER working paper, 2006).
[†]D.J. Koehler and C.S.K. Poon, "Self-Predictions Overweight Strength of Current Intentions," *Journal of Experimental Social Psychology* 42 (2006): 517–524.

In general, people were massively too optimistic about their blood donation.

Those who scored themselves a 9 thought they were about 90 percent likely to give blood; however, only 40 percent of them did so. Those who scored themselves a 5 thought they were around 45 percent likely to give blood, but less than 20 percent of them actually did so. Those who had low current intentions (scoring themselves a 2) thought they were 10 percent likely to give blood and not one of them did. The predicted probability of blood donation rose much faster across the strength of current intentions than the actual outcome. This implies that current intentions have an overly strong effect on prediction of behavior, but not on behavior itself. That is to say, we all think we will be good in the future, but we won't be!

So how do we overcome this hurdle? When it comes to food, Wansink says that a combination of rebiasing and simple rules can help us. For instance, using a smaller size plate can help turn framing to our advantage—as obviously a smaller plate looks full with less than a large plate. Simple rules such as half of the plate should be vegetables, remember to slow down (start last and finish last), or drink no more than one sugared soft drink, are all examples which will eventually lead to good habits.

Wansink also suggests trying to alter no more than three aspects of our behavior at one time; we simply can't cope with too many changes at once. I could go on the cabbage soup diet, and I would almost certainly lose weight (not to mention friends), but as soon as I came off the diet I would probably start to put weight back on again. Small manageable steps are likely to be the best way towards sustainable weight loss. The same is likely to be true when it comes to investing. We shouldn't try to change everything in one swoop, as we'll fail. Working out which biases you suffer from the most, and addressing these first, should help improve returns.

Over the course of this book I've tried to suggest ways in which you can protect yourself against the most common mental pitfalls and shown you the ways in which some of the world's best investors have put processes in place to defend themselves.

The key lesson from these investors is that we must concentrate on process. Process is the set of rules that govern how we go about investing. As we have seen time and time again in this Little Book, some of the worlds greatest investors (from Sir John Templeton's research on a quiet day to George Soros's diaries, from Bruce Berkowitz's kill the company to Michael Steinhardt's selling the entire portfolio) have integrated measures into the way in which they approach investment to act as a guard against mindless investing. The reason they have codi-fied the process is that they know that unless they force themselves to behave in this fashion, they will slip back into old habits.

So think carefully about the way you invest. Which of these errors have you committed most regularly? What might you be able to do to prevent yourself from stumbling down this path again? Thinking about these issues is the first step in overcoming your own worst enemy when it comes to investment—yourself!